have come to dedicate a portion of that field as a final resting place for those who here gave their lives that that nation might live. ★ ★It is altogether fitting and proper that we should do this. ★ ★But in a larger sense we cannot dedicate, we cannot consecrate, we cannot hallow this ground. ★ The brave men, living and dead, who struggled here, have consecrated it far above our poor power to add or detract. The world will little note, nor long remember, what we say here, but it can never forget what they did here. ★ ★It is for us, the living, rather to be dedicated here to the unfinished work which they who fought here have thus far so nobly advanced It is rather for us to be here dedicated to the great task remaining before us, that from these honored dead we take increased devotion to that cause for which they gave the last full measure of devotion; ★ that we here highly resolve that these dead shall not have died in vain; that this nation, under God, shall have a new birth of freedom, and that the government of the people, by the people, and for the people, shall not perish from the earth.

GETTYSBURG

GETTYSBURG

THE TURNING POINT IN THE STRUGGLE BETWEEN NORTH AND SOUTH

KEVIN J. DOUGHERTY

METRO BOOKS
NEW YORK

METRO BOOKS
New York

An Imprint of Sterling Publishing
387 Park Avenue South
New York, NY 10016

Editorial and design by
Amber Books Ltd
74–77 White Lion Street
London N1 9PF
www.amberbooks.co.uk

Project Editor: Michael Spilling
Designer: Jerry Williams
Picture Research: Terry Forshaw

ISBN: 978-1-4351-4622-8

For information about custom editions, special sales, and premium and corporate purchases, please
contact Sterling Special Sales at 800-805-5489 or specialsales@sterlingpublishing.com.

Manufactured in China

2 4 6 8 10 9 7 5 3 1

www.sterlingpublishing.com

Contents

Introduction

As the new year of 1863 dawned, there was little about Gettysburg, Pennsylvania to lead one to believe that before the summer was over, the small town would be transformed to the site of perhaps the most important battle of the Civil War and certainly its most costly. The town was founded in the 1780s and named after James Gettys. With Gettys as its visionary, Gettysburg grew steadily. It was incorporated in 1806 and became the seat of Adams County. As a rural market town, it was the junction of several roads, and it was this feature that would catapult Gettysburg to its permanent place of significance in the history of the United States.

General Robert E. Lee had become a problem for which President Abraham Lincoln had yet to find a solution. Upon assuming command of the Army of Northern Virginia in 1862, Lee had thwarted Major General George McClellan's drive to Richmond during the Peninsula Campaign (March–July 1862). On the strength of that victory, Lee then humiliated Major General John Pope at Second Manassas (August 28–30, 1862). Hoping to decisively turn the tide

of the war, Lee marched into Maryland where McClellan battled him to a tactical draw but strategic victory at Antietam (September 17, 1862). The Federal respite was short-lived when Lee next defeated Major General Ambrose Burnside at Fredericksburg (December 11–15, 1862). Lincoln replaced Burnside with Major General Joseph Hooker who Lee mastered at Chancellorsville (April 30–May 6, 1863).

As Lee plotted his second invasion of Northern territory, he would have to do so without his most trusted subordinate, Lieutenant General Thomas "Stonewall" Jackson. Jackson's death at Chancellorsville would force Lee to reorganize his army and elevate to corps command officers who had performed ably at the division level but would prove not yet ready for additional responsibilities. Jackson would be sorely missed, and Lee would later muse, "If I [had] had Stonewall Jackson at Gettysburg, I would have won that fight."

RIGHT: Major General George Meade was thrust into a position he did not desire as commander of the Army of the Potomac, but he rose to the occasion at Gettysburg.

Lee's Gamble

In addition to the absence of Jackson, there were other factors that would make an invasion of the North a gamble for the Confederates. Even the great victory at Chancellorsville had cost Lee 12,821 casualties or 22 percent of his total force. Many thought it unwise to go on a strategic offensive and further risk the limited manpower available to the Army of Northern Virginia. Perhaps the most vociferous of those advocating the defensive was Lee's "Old War Horse," Lieutenant General James Longstreet. Longstreet reported that "almost every day from the 10th May 1863 until the Battle [of Gettysburg]," he and Lee discussed strategy. Longstreet consistently argued the strength of the defensive and would continue this position even after the battle was joined. Others saw the threat to Lieutenant General John Pemberton's beleaguered force at Vicksburg, Mississippi as being a priority and felt that instead of mounting its own offensive, the Army of Northern Virginia should be sent to reinforce the Confederacy in the west.

Lee countered these arguments, positing that his attacking north would actually help Pemberton by diverting Federal attention away from Vicksburg. Moreover, Lee, who maintained intense loyalty to his native state, saw a campaign into Northern territory as an opportunity to give Virginia a brief respite from the ravages of war. Finally, if Lee could gain a decisive victory, there was a possibility of gaining the tantalizing foreign recognition that had thus far eluded the Confederacy and perhaps motivate the Union to seek a negotiated peace.

Even more basic to Lee's strategic thinking was his core commitment to the Napoleonic tradition and its predominance of offensive action. According to this philosophy, wars were won by attacking, and the defensive was only a temporary expedient to create conditions to assume the attack. Indeed, staff officer Colonel Joseph Ives observed, "Lee is audacity. His name is audacity." Emboldening this strategic belief was Lee's unshakeable faith in his men. Indeed, writing in retrospect some 14 years after the battle, Major General Henry Heth would state, "The fact is, General Lee believed the Army of Northern Virginia, as it then existed, could accomplish anything."

New Commander

On the Federal side, Major General George Meade did not enjoy such a confident demeanor. Thrust into command of the Army of the Potomac only after Lee had already begun his march north, Meade asked "Why me?" Meade can be forgiven for such musings. He had inherited no plan and did not even know the whereabouts of all the elements of his command, let alone where Lee was and what his intentions were. What Meade did know was that whether

RIGHT: While Lee argued for an invasion of the North, others worried about the deteriorating situation at Vicksburg, where 33,000 Confederate soldiers were beseiged.

he wanted the responsibility or not, the fate of the Union now rested on his shoulders.

Thus the stage was set for the clash of the two armies. It was a battle in which Lee was willing to risk much in order to win. Conversely it was one in which Meade would play it safe so as not to lose. On July 1, small elements of each side stumbled upon each other in a "meeting engagement" west of Gettysburg. The outcome of that day's fighting would be decided largely by which side could rush forward their

reinforcements fastest. The Confederates won that race and could claim victory on the first day.

In spite of Longstreet's reiteration of his arguments to assume a defensive posture, Lee developed a plan to attack on the second day. By this time the Federal line had assumed its famous "fish hook" shape with Little Round Top on the southern flank. Only a herculean effort by Colonel Strong Vincent and the heroics of Lieutenant Colonel Joshua Chamberlain saved this key terrain for the Federals. With the

Confederates denied this ability to roll up the Federal flank, the second day ended in a stalemate. Lee, again overruling a despondent Longstreet, decided to renew the attack on July 3. The result was the famous "Pickett's Charge," which for many defines the three-day battle. The bravery of the Confederate soldiers could not overcome the firepower advantage of rifles and artillery, and the third day was a decisive Federal victory. Lee was left with no other choice but to withdraw back to Virginia. Even in victory, the Army of the Potomac was badly bruised, and

Meade, to the chagrin of President Abraham Lincoln, was content to let Lee slip away quietly.

Lee's gamble had been a costly one and the casualties incurred at Gettysburg prevented the Army of Northern Virginia from ever again going on the offensive. The twin defeat at Vicksburg was doubly damaging to the Confederacy. Still the Federal forces were not able to end the war until Lieutenant General Ulysses S. Grant became general-in-chief, and, with Major General William Sherman, implemented a strategy to press the Confederates

simultaneously on all fronts. Nonetheless, for many, Gettysburg represented the "High Watermark of the Confederacy."

The battlefield quickly became enshrined as hallowed ground in the American experience with the dedication of the Soldiers' National Cemetery (also known as Gettysburg National Cemetery) and Lincoln's Gettysburg Address. Today over a million people visit the battlefield each year, and the story of Gettysburg continues to be told in films, articles, and books. This present volume hopes to contribute to this legacy by combining narrative, maps, photographs, and primary source documents to provide a neutral and balanced account of this pivotal moment in American history. The book begins with an outline of the formative stages of the campaign from its evolution after Chancellorsville to Lee's movement north into Pennsylvania. Each of the three days is then discussed in detail, followed by an analysis of the aftermath of the battle. The book ends with brief biographical descriptions of the key participants on both sides. All these sections are punctuated with excerpts from letters, diaries, and official reports of participants so the reader can experience and interpret the history through the words of those who made it.

LEFT: Today, a host of monuments such as this one commemorating the 111th New York Infantry bears silent sentinel over the battlefield.

FACING PAGE: The bucolic countryside of Gettysburg belies the carnage that descended there in July 1863.

The Campaign

The Gettysburg Campaign marked Lee's second invasion of the North. It was risky in that it stretched the limited offensive capability of the Army of Northern Virginia and the already thinly distributed resources of the Confederacy, but it offered Lee the tantalizing possibility of a decisive victory.

Perhaps the most well-known battle of the Civil War, the Battle of Gettysburg was fought between General Robert E. Lee's Army of Northern Virginia and Major General George Meade's Army of the Potomac. Gettysburg was Lee's second invasion of the North and another effort to gain the decisive victory that would perhaps lead to European intervention or a negotiated peace. Instead, Meade defeated Lee in a three-day battle that forced Lee back into Virginia and eliminated the Army of Northern Virginia as a future offensive threat.

The Battle of Gettysburg was part of a larger campaign that began shortly after the Confederate victory at Chancellorsville (April 30–May 6, 1863). Campaigns are "a series of related major operations aimed at achieving strategic and operational objectives within a given time and space." Battles are "a set of related engagements that lasts longer and involves larger forces than an engagement."

FACING PAGE: Although a simplified view of the Confederate army deploying, this painting by John Richards does give some idea of the rolling fields, broken bywoods, farm houses, and creeks that defined the Gettysburg battlefield.

RIGHT: Joseph Hooker was in command of the Army of the Potomac at the beginning of the Gettysburg Campaign.

Engagements are "a tactical conflict, usually between opposing, lower echelon maneuver forces."

The Gettysburg Campaign began when Lee initiated his move north on June 3. It ended on July 14 when the Army of Northern Virginia returned to Virginia. Within that campaign, the three days from July 1 to July 3 comprise the Battle of Gettysburg. Within that battle, a host of engagements occurred at places like Culp's Hill, Devil's Den, and Little Round Top.

The Campaign Takes Shape

On May 1, 1863 Lee launched an attack on Chancellorsville that dealt a devastating blow to Major General Joseph Hooker and the Army of the Potomac. Although the battle was a great victory for the Confederates, it proved to be a costly one with the loss of Lieutenant General Stonewall Jackson. Previously Lee had had two corps commanders with Jackson leading one corps and Lieutenant General James Longstreet leading the other. Each corps had some 30,000 men, and Lee felt that with Jackson gone there was no one commander who could replace him and manage a unit that large. Instead, Lee

RIGHT: At the same time Lee was contemplating his invasion of Pennsylvania, Confederate forces at Vicksburg were hard pressed. Ultimately John Pemberton (right) surrendered to Ulysses Grant (left) there.

FACING PAGE: The Battle of Chancellorsville left the Federal Army of the Potomac in a command crisis and the momentum with the Army of Northern Virginia.

reorganized the Army of Northern Virginia into three corps. Longstreet would command one, Lieutenant General Dick Ewell would take Jackson's old Second Corps, and Lieutenant General A. P. Hill would command the new Third Corps. Ewell and Hill had both served

ably as division commanders, but it remained to be seen if they were up to the challenge of corps command.

Chancellorsville had left the Federal army of the Potomac reeling, and Lee proposed a second invasion of Northern territory to build on this

momentum. Complicating such a move, however, was the fact that at the beginning of 1863, the Confederacy was faced with two completely different situations in the eastern and western theaters. The Confederate success in the east was reversed in the western theater where Major General Ulysses S. Grant posed a mounting threat to Lieutenant General John Pemberton's beleaguered command at Vicksburg and the Confederacy's ability to maintain some control over the strategically important Mississippi River.

On May 19, Secretary of War James Seddon, encouraged by the likes of Longstreet, General Pierre Goustave Toutant Beauregard, and Senator Louis Wigfall, asked Lee for his thoughts on sending one of his divisions west.

EXCERPT FROM "GENERAL JAMES LONGSTREET'S ACCOUNT OF THE CAMPAIGN AND BATTLE"

Passing through Richmond, I called to pay my respects to Mr. Seddon, the Secretary of War. Mr. Seddon was at the time of my visit deeply considering the critical condition of Pemberton's army at Vicksburg, around which Gen. Grant was then decisively drawing his lines. He informed me that he had in contemplation a plan for concentrating a succoring army at Jackson, Miss., under the command of General Johnston, with a view of driving Grant from before Vicksburg by a direct issue at arms. He suggested that possibly my corps might be needed to make the army strong enough to handle Grant, and asked me my views. I replied that there was a better plan, in my judgment, for relieving Vicksburg than by a direct assault upon Grant. I proposed that the army then concentrating at Jackson, Miss., be moved swiftly to Tullahoma, where General Bragg was then located with a fine army, confronting an army of about equal strength, under General Rosecranz, and that at the same time the two divisions of my corps be hurried forward to the same point. The simultaneous arrival of these reinforcements would give us a grand army at Tullahoma. With this army General Johnston might speedily crush Rosecranz, and that he should then turn his force toward the north, and with his splendid army march through Tennessee and Kentucky, and threaten the invasion of Ohio. My idea was, that in the march through those States the army would meet no organized obstruction; would be supplied with provisions, and even reinforcements, by those friendly to our cause, and would inevitably result in drawing Grant's army from Vicksburg to look after and protect his own territory. Mr. Seddon adhered to his original views; not so much, I think, from his great confidence in them as from the difficulty of withdrawing the force suggested from General Lee's army.

ABOVE: Robert E. Lee's impressive string of victories, including Fredericksburg as shown here, had brought him much prestige in the Confederacy and created much anxiety in the Union.

FACING PAGE: Accidentally shot by one of his own men, Stonewall Jackson's death at Chancellorsville cost Lee the irreplaceable services of his best corps commander and his right-hand man.

BELOW: President Jefferson Davis did not rely too heavily on the advice of his secretaries of war, including James Seddon who is shown here.

For Lee, the discussion boiled down to "a question between Virginia and the Mississippi."

Indeed, Lee's loyalties had always been first and foremost to Virginia. Shortly after resigning from the U.S. Army he said, "I devote myself to the service of my native state, in whose behalf alone, will I ever again draw my sword." This loyalty had a profound influence on Lee's strategic thinking and now an invasion into Northern territory would relieve some of the ravages Virginia had suffered as the principal battleground of the war.

There were others who looked to the western theater as being the more important theater. This "western bloc" advocated sending reinforcements from Virginia west to help Pemberton instead of mounting an offensive in the eastern theater. Lee countered these arguments, saying that an invasion of the North would cause such alarm that the Federals would be forced to divert their attention away from Vicksburg. It was a fairly tenuous assertion, but by this point in the war Lee had such enormous prestige that his opinions were hard to ignore. When Lee presented his plan to invade Northern territory to President Davis and his cabinet on May 15, 1863, Davis concurred and the question was settled.

Plans for a Northern Invasion

The initiation of the Gettysburg Campaign can be traced to June 3, when Lee started moving his 89,000 men north from an assembly point at Culpeper, some 30 miles (50 km) northwest of

EXCERPT FROM LEE'S LETTER TO HIS WIFE NOTING STUART'S REVIEW

CULPEPER
June 9, 1863

... I reviewed the cavalry in this section yesterday. It was a splendid sight. The men and horses looked well. They had recuperated since last fall. Stuart was in all his glory. The country here looks very green and pretty, notwithstanding the ravages of war. What a beautiful world God, in his loving kindness to his creatures, has given us. What a shame that men, endowed with reason and a knowledge of right, should mar his gifts.

Truly & affly yours
R. E. LEE

Fredericksburg. Paying close attention to the security of his army and the secrecy of the move, Lee shifted two-thirds of his force to the northwest and past Hooker's flank. Lee left Lieutenant General A. P. Hill's corps entrenched around Fredericksburg, spread out to give the impression the entire army was still there. Lee also used Major General Jeb Stuart's cavalry to hold the passes in the Blue Ridge and South mountains to screen the army's advance and protect its supply line. Then Lee quietly began moving westward up the Shenandoah and Cumberland valleys.

Hooker was still stinging from his defeat at Chancellorsville, and he proceeded cautiously given his uncertainty of the situation. After taking command of the army, Hooker had initiated several administrative reforms including a reorganization of the Bureau of Military Information under Colonel George Sharpe. The improvements in the Federal intelligence arm had been significant, and as early as May 27, Sharpe was reporting that "the Confederate army is under marching orders" and would probably "move forward upon or above our right flank." Balloon observers also noted departures, and on June 4 Sharpe reported, "There is a considerable movement of the enemy. Their camps are disappearing at some points."

On June 5–6, Hooker sent a division from Major General John Sedgwick's VI Corps across the Rappahannock River just downstream from Fredericksburg to investigate these reports. Hill's men resisted strongly and blocked Sedgwick's advance, but by now Hooker was convinced Lee was on the move. He suggested to President Abraham Lincoln that, now that Lee was gone, the Federals could take Richmond. "I am of the opinion," Hooker wrote Lincoln, "that it is my duty to pitch into [Lee's] rear." On June 10, Lincoln silenced such thinking, responding that

RIGHT: Both sides used balloons to conduct aerial reconnaissance of enemy positions, but intelligence reports were not always well-analyzed and synthesized with other information.

"I think Lee's army, and not Richmond, is your true objective point."

Still uncertain how to proceed, Hooker sought more intelligence. He had received reports of Confederate cavalry massing around Culpeper in anticipation of some sort of raid. He told Lincoln of his "great desire to 'bust it up' before it got fairly under way." Indeed, Stuart did represent a force to be reckoned with. He had five brigades of cavalry and six batteries of horse artillery for a combined total of 10,292 men. On June 4, the flamboyant Stuart held a opulent ball to celebrate the grand review to be held the next day. Stuart held a more military review on June 8 which Lee attended.

Brandy Station

His preliminaries complete, Stuart readied to cross the Rappahannock on June 9 to begin screening Lee's advance. He bivouacked on Fleetwood Hill overlooking Brandy Station, blissfully unaware that Hooker had dispatched Major General Alfred Pleasonton's Cavalry Corps "to disperse and destroy" the Confederate

LEFT: Hooker was just the latest commander of the Army of the Potomac that President Abraham Lincoln found hard to energize. George McClellan, shown here with Lincoln at Antietam, had been particularly vexing.

FACING PAGE: A. P. Hill provided a staunch defense against John Sedgwick's attack across the Rappahannock, as illustrated and annotated in this drawing from shortly after the battle.

cavalry reported to be "assembled in the vicinity of Culpeper." Pleasonton had massed his men opposite Beverly Ford, 4 miles (6.5 km) northeast of Brandy Station, and Kelly Ford, 5 miles (8 km) southeast, with orders to cross the Rappahannock at "earliest dawn" or 4:30 a.m. With just one company of the 6th Virginia Cavalry patrolling the river bank near Beverly Ford, most of Stuart's men enjoyed a "last sweet snooze" while Pleasonton's 7,900 cavalry and 3,000 infantry prepared to attack.

Brigadier General John Buford initiated the attack from his assembly area at Beverly Ford. As Colonel Benjamin Franklin Davis's men splashed across the Rappahannock, they brushed aside the weak Confederate defenses. Davis was killed in the attack, but his men raced on down the road to Brandy Station. The left wing of the Federal attack launched from Kelly's Ford was less successful. Both Colonel Alfred Duffie and Brigadier General David Gregg experienced delays that left Buford to carry the lion's share of the Federal effort.

As Buford advanced, he ran into Brigadier General William "Grumble" Jones's brigade forming a line near St. James Church. Both sides hurried to rush reinforcements to this location, and a succession of charges and countercharges ensued. Stuart was at the scene of this fighting when he received the alarming news that a Federal column was also approaching Brandy

Station, in the rear of the Confederate line at St. James Church. This was the delayed attack of Gregg, and Stuart frantically ordered a counterattack by Brigadier General Wade Hampton to meet it. Hampton arrived just in time, and by noon Pleasonton realized that his two wings would not be able to unite. A few

FACING PAGE: Edwin Forbes rendered this dramatic drawing of the cavalry Battle of Brandy Station.

BELOW: By the time of the Civil War, traditional cavalry charges such as at Brandy Station were rare. However, another would occur on the third day of the Battle of Gettysburg.

BELOW: Alfred Pleasonton (seated center), shown here with his staff and officers, helped breathe new life into the Federal cavalry with its performance at Brandy Station.

hours later he ordered Buford and Gregg to fall back to the Rappahannock crossings.

Stuart may have retained control of the field and claimed victory, but his reputation certainly suffered. The *Charleston Mercury* described Brandy Station as an "ugly surprise," and the *Daily Richmond Examiner* reported that "Gen.

Stuart has suffered no little in public estimation by the late enterprises of the enemy." Numerous observers would later explain Stuart's subsequent conduct during the campaign as an effort to recover what he had lost at Brandy Station.

Pleasonton also claimed success, arguing that his "reconnaissance" had uncovered Lee's plan

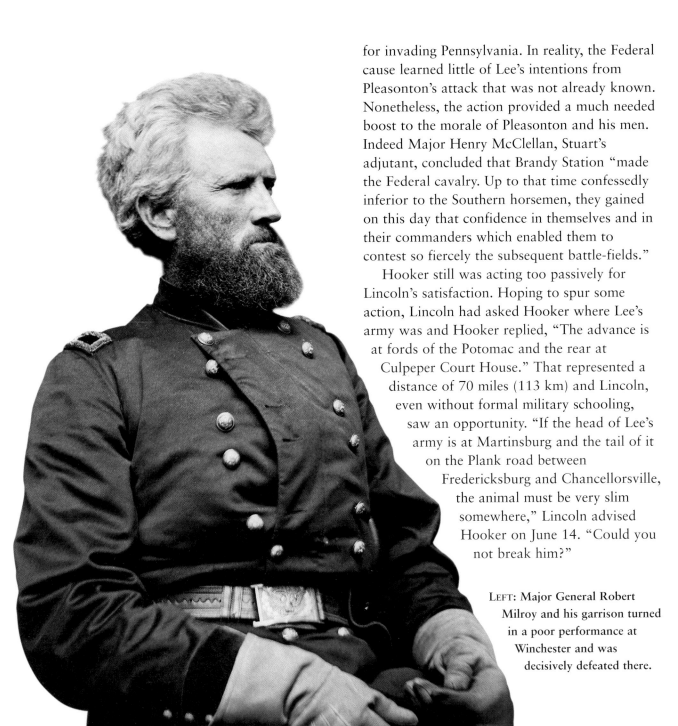

LEFT: Major General Robert
Milroy and his garrison turned
in a poor performance at
Winchester and was
decisively defeated there.

for invading Pennsylvania. In reality, the Federal cause learned little of Lee's intentions from Pleasonton's attack that was not already known. Nonetheless, the action provided a much needed boost to the morale of Pleasonton and his men. Indeed Major Henry McClellan, Stuart's adjutant, concluded that Brandy Station "made the Federal cavalry. Up to that time confessedly inferior to the Southern horsemen, they gained on this day that confidence in themselves and in their commanders which enabled them to contest so fiercely the subsequent battle-fields."

Hooker still was acting too passively for Lincoln's satisfaction. Hoping to spur some action, Lincoln had asked Hooker where Lee's army was and Hooker replied, "The advance is at fords of the Potomac and the rear at Culpeper Court House." That represented a distance of 70 miles (113 km) and Lincoln, even without formal military schooling, saw an opportunity. "If the head of Lee's army is at Martinsburg and the tail of it on the Plank road between Fredericksburg and Chancellorsville, the animal must be very slim somewhere," Lincoln advised Hooker on June 14. "Could you not break him?"

Lee's Planned Offensive

While Hooker and Lincoln exchanged telegrams, Lee was moving. On the afternoon of June 10, he had started Ewell's Second Corps up the Shenandoah Valley and by June 13 the divisions of Major Generals Edward Johnson and Jubal Early were closing in on Winchester. There Major General Robert Milroy commanded a garrison of 5,100 Federals that Lee could ill-afford to leave in his rear as he marched north. Major General Henry Halleck had earlier tried unsuccessfully to get Milroy to relocate from this vulnerable position to Harper's Ferry, 30 miles (50 km) to the northeast, and now it was too late.

On June 14, Ewell attacked. Milroy belatedly tried to evacuate to Harper's Ferry, but Ewell had anticipated that move and blocked the route. Milroy still had superior numbers, but he squandered them in piecemeal attacks until Confederate reinforcements could arrive. When the fighting was over, the Federals had suffered 443 casualties and had 3,358 men, 23 guns, and 300 wagons captured. The Confederates had incurred only 269 casualties.

Geographical Considerations

On June 15, Lee ordered Longstreet and Hill's corps forward. While Longstreet was on the move, Lee ordered him to help Stuart, who had left Brandy Station on June 16, plug the gaps in the Blue Ridge Mountains to screen Hill's march. Screening operations protect a force from enemy observation, and as Lee advanced north, he took

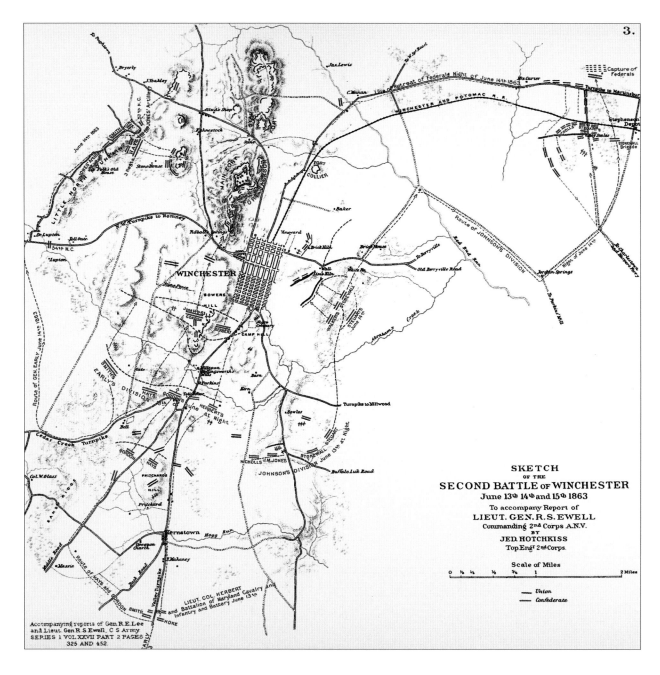

SKETCH
OF THE
SECOND BATTLE OF WINCHESTER
June 13th 14th and 15th 1863
To accompany Report of
LIEUT. GEN. R. S. EWELL
Commanding 2nd Corps A.N.V.
BY
JED. HOTCHKISS
Top Engr 2nd Corps.

Scale of Miles

—— Union
—— Confederate

advantage of the lay of the land to conceal his movements.

Three parallel ranges, the Blue Ridge, Allegheny, and Bull Run mountains, ran north by northeast, cutting through central Virginia to the Potomac River, across Maryland and then into Pennsylvania. To the west, the Shenandoah Valley lay between the Alleghenies and the Blue Ridge. To the east, the Blue Ridge and Bull Run framed the Loudoun Valley. Ashby's Gap, Thoroughfare Gap, Aldie's Gap, and various other passes had to be controlled for Lee to have safe passage.

The terrain was familiar to the Confederates. Jackson had used the Shenandoah Valley to defeat three numerically superior Federal forces in 1862 and Lee had used the Loudoun Valley as his approach to the Battle of Second Manassas. As part of the screening effort, a series of skirmishes were fought between June 17 and 21, but the Confederates kept Pleasonton from breaking through.

Stuart's Ride
After Stuart accomplished his screening mission in the Valley, Lee had originally planned on the cavalry accompanying the army into

LEFT: Geography and a lack of intelligence helped the Federals be surrounded and defeated at Winchester.

FACING PAGE: The Shenandoah Valley, cutting a north-south passage through northern Virginia, was important as an agricultural area and an invasion route.

Pennsylvania. Instead, at a June 18 meeting with Lee in the small village of Paris, just east of Ashby's Gap, Stuart suggested he be allowed to harass Hooker in order to delay the Federal army's pursuit. Lee acquiesced and made the mistake of giving Stuart broad latitude in supporting the Confederate advance north. Stuart would use this discretion to leave only a small part of his force screening Lee and lead the rest of his men on a broad sweep around Hooker's rear in hopes of repeating the same havoc inflicted against Major General George McClellan during the Peninsula Campaign.

In so doing, Stuart had expected to be out of contact with Lee for just 36 hours. Instead, Stuart would be forced to loop much further east than he had anticipated and would not rejoin Lee for a full week. With Stuart gone, Lee would be without his prized intelligence asset and thus be painfully unaware of Federal troop dispositions. It would prove to be a costly mistake for Lee.

In the meantime, Lee's infantry moved forward. Ewell's divisions had crossed the Potomac near Shepherdstown between June 15 and June 18. Hill's corps started crossing there on June 25 and Longstreet the same day at Williamsport. The crossing was completed on

FACING PAGE: As Stuart screened Lee's northern advance, Confederate and Federal cavalry clashed at places like Middleburg on June 17–19 (top) and Upperville on June 21 (bottom), Virginia. Both were cavalry engagements involving minor casualties.

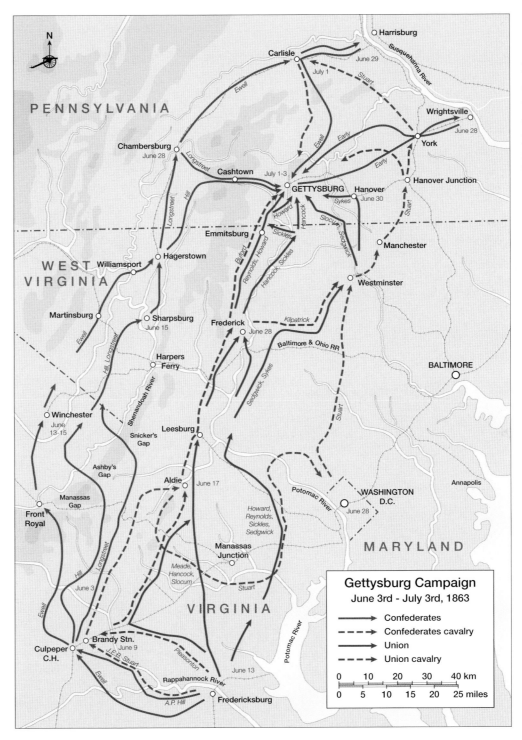

LEFT: As Lee advanced north, the Federal Army of the Potomac paralleled his route to guard Washington and Baltimore.

Gettysburg Campaign
June 3rd - July 3rd, 1863

———▶ Confederates
- - - ▶ Confederates cavalry
———▶ Union
- - - ▶ Union cavalry

0 10 20 30 40 km
0 5 10 15 20 25 miles

June 26 and the two corps reunited at Hagerstown and began moving toward Chambersburg with Hill in the lead. Lee personally crossed on June 25.

The Confederates March North

The marching was hard, but not particularly dangerous. Maryland was a slave state with a considerable number of Confederate sympathizers. Many people gathered along the route of march to gain a glimpse of the Army of Northern Virginia and particularly Lee. As the story goes, even a Northern girl waving an American flag was overheard to say as Lee passed by, "Oh, I wish he was ours."

Lee continued his advance north virtually unopposed, and once in Pennsylvania, the Army of Northern Virginia began to enjoy the bounty of the countryside. A few communities were forced to pay cash ransoms or provide some sort of tribute. Greencastle was the first of these, and Confederates demanded 120 pistols, 100 saddles and bridles, 1,000 pounds (450 kg) of leather, 2,000 pounds (900 kg) of lead, 200 currycombs, 12 boxes of tin, and assorted foodstuffs there. The town council had little means of acting on such a request, and the Confederates proceeded to collect what they found or were given and then

FACING PAGE: Lee had earlier invaded the north in 1862 and the two armies clashed at Antietam, Maryland, in September of that year. Antietam was the bloodiest single day of the war; Confederate casualties were such that Lee had to curtail his invasion of the North.

marched on. This procedure was indicative of the main body of Lee's army. Lee endeavored to keep a firm hand on his men, insisting Confederate money or receipts be issued for anything taken.

Generally his troops took what they could without resorting to violence. The exceptions most often came from less disciplined cavalrymen. The region had already had some experience

EXCERPT FROM *THREE MONTHS IN THE SOUTHERN STATES* BY ARTHUR FREMANTLE (A BRITISH OBSERVER TRAVELING WITH LEE'S ARMY)

June 29, 1863

We are still at Chambersburg. Lee has issued a remarkably good order on non-retaliation, which is generally well received; but I have heard of complaints from fire-eaters, who want vengeance for their wrongs; and when one considers the numbers of officers and soldiers with this army who have been totally ruined by the devastations of Northern troops, one cannot be much surprised at this feeling.

I went into Chambersburg again, and witnessed the singular good behavior of the troops towards the citizens. I heard soldiers saying to one another, that they did not like being in a town in which they were very naturally detested. To any one who has seen as I have the ravages of the Northern troops in Southern towns, this forbearance seems most commendable and surprising. Yet these Pennsylvania Dutch don't seem the least thankful, and really appear to be unaware that their own troops have been for two years

treating Southern towns with ten times more harshness. They are the most unpatriotic people I ever saw, and openly state that they don't care which side wins, provided they are left alone. They abuse Lincoln tremendously.

Of course, in such a large army as this there must be many instances of bad characters, who are always ready to plunder and pillage whenever they can do so without being caught: the stragglers, also, who remain behind when the army has left, will doubtless do much harm. It is impossible to prevent this; but every thing that can be done is done to protect private property and non-combatants, and I can say, from my own observation, with wonderful success. I hear instances, however, in which soldiers, meeting well-dressed citizens, have made a "long arm" and changed hats, much to the disgust of the latter, who are still more annoyed when an exchange of boots is also proposed: their superfine broadcloth is never in any danger.

RIGHT: After Chancellorsville, Darius Couch had been reassigned from the Army of the Potomac and given command of the Department of the Susquehanna.

with invasion. Lee's first venture into Northern territory in September 1862 had brought the fighting to Antietam Creek in Maryland, barely 50 miles (80 km) from Gettysburg. A month later, Stuart led a force of 1,800 men that crossed the Potomac River on October 9 and reached Chambersburg that night. There he destroyed a machine shop and many public stores before bivouacking in the streets of the town. At daybreak the next morning, he departed with 500 captured horses. He passed Emmitsburg on the afternoon of October 11 and recrossed the Potomac the next day. According to one newspaper account, Stuart's men had been seen at Latshaw's Tavern, barely 4 miles (6.5 km) to the west of Gettysburg.

All told, Stuart had covered 126 miles (200 km) and demonstrated to the Pennsylvanians that they were not immune to the reach of Confederate cavalry. As a result of such experiences, 13-year-old Billy Bayly recalled that "living near the border line . . . with frequent alarms as to guerilla raids, we 'skedaddled' on various occasions with a view to saving our horses." This latest

advance of the entire Army of Northern Virginia, however, understandably created more tension among the local population.

Typical of this new sense of urgency was a June 15 entry in the diary of Sallie Broadhead in which she recorded the arrival of a telegram from Governor Andrew Curtin advising Gettysburg citizens to move their stores to more secure places as quickly as possible. Another message from Harrisburg on June 20 asked for volunteers to help defend the state's capital city. More worrisome was an announcement the same day by Major General Darius Couch, commander of the Department of the Susquehanna, that residents should see to their own protection. As a result, a meeting was called for the purpose of "placing the county in a state of military organization as would be deemed most advisable."

The Confederates Reach Gettysburg

The advance of the Confederate army was signaled by an influx of refugees crossing South Mountain from the Cumberland Valley into Adams County. The citizens of southern Pennsylvania braced themselves as a newspaper article in the *Sentinel* predicted that "a great battle will be fought . . . a collision is almost

FACING PAGE: Contrary to these illustrations from a Northern magazine showing Confederate troops looting in Chambersburg, most of Lee's infantrymen were disciplined in their interactions with the citizens of Pennsylvania.

THE REBEL FORAY IN PENNSYLVANIA—GENERAL VIEW OF CHAMBERSBURG.—Sketched by Mr. Davis.—[See Page 698.]

THE REBELS EXCHANGING THEIR RAGS FOR U. S. ARMY OVERCOATS AT CHAMBERSBURG, PA.—[Sketched by Mr. Davis.]   BURNING THE ENGINE HOUSE AND MACHINE SHOPS AT CHAMBERSBURG, PA.—Sketched by Mr. Davis.—[See Page 698.]

certain." Many, however, considered Harrisburg or Philadelphia to be more likely targets for the Confederate attack than a sleepy town like Gettysburg. One citizen confessed, "We thought the bulk of the Union soldiers were far away . . . and no one dreamed of a battle being fought in our town." Another wondered, "what would the rebels ever want to come to Gettysburg for?" Armed with such logic, the residents of Gettysburg seemed completely unaware that two massive armies, altogether about 170,000 men, were converging on their town. There might be an artillery exchange "or something of that kind," but as Jennie McCreary wrote to her sister, Julia, "We never expected a battle."

Such denials increasingly were at odds with events unfolding on the ground. On the afternoon of June 26, Early's 5,000 veteran troops approached Gettysburg. Opposing them was the 26th Pennsylvania Emergency Volunteers, an untested militia unit mustered into service only on June 19. With less than a week of any kind of military training, the would-be defenders had arrived at Gettysburg just a day before Early. When confronted by the vastly superior Confederate force, the Pennsylvanians were quickly routed. Many were captured and then paroled. Still they

LEFT: Taken shortly after the Civil War, this photograph shows a section of raised rail track at Hanover, Pennsylvania. On June 30, Stuart's and Kilpatrick's cavalry fought an inconclusive battle there.

ABOVE: New to corps command, Dick Ewell would prove cautious at Gettysburg, and not showing the boldness that Lee's strategy required to be successful.

could claim to be the first organized defenders of Pennsylvania soil in the face of this new invasion.

With this token resistance brushed aside, the Confederates proceeded to enter Gettysburg through the Chambersburg Pike. Early demanded such produce as sugar, coffee, flour, salt, bacon, onions, and whiskey; 1,000 pairs of shoes; 500 hats; and $5,000 in cash. David Kendlehart, President of the Town Council, told

Early the town could not provide such quantities, but promised that stores and shops would remain open for trade. In fact, the notice of the Confederate advance had been sufficient for many residents to hide or remove their prized belongings. Early was in a hurry to proceed to York, some 30 miles (50 km) away, and he had time only for the most cursory search of Gettysburg. What amount of his requested items he actually secured is uncertain.

York surrendered to Early the evening of June 27. From there the Confederate

LINCOLN'S PROCLAMATION CALLING VARIOUS STATE MILITIAS INTO SERVICE

WAR DEPARTMENT
June 15, 1863

By the President of the United States of America
A PROCLAMATION

Whereas the armed insurrectionary combinations now existing in several of the States are threatening to make inroads into the States of Maryland, West Virginia, Pennsylvania, and Ohio, requiring immediately an additional force for the service of the United States: Now, therefore, I, Abraham Lincoln, President of the United States, and Commander-in-Chief of the Army and Navy thereof, and of the militia of the several States when called into actual service, do hereby call into the service of the United States 100,000 militia from the States following, namely: From the State of Maryland, 10,000; from the State of Pennsylvania, 50,000; from the State of Ohio, 30,000; from the State of West Virginia, 10,000; to be mustered into the service of the United States forth with, and to serve for the period of six

months from the date of such muster into said service, unless sooner discharged; to be mustered in as infantry, artillery, and cavalry, in proportions which will be made known through the War Department, which Department will also designate the several places of rendezvous. These militia to be organized according to the rules and regulations of the volunteer service, and such orders as may hereafter be issued. The States aforesaid will be respectively under the enrollment act for the militia service rendered under this proclamation. In testimony whereof, I have hereunto set my hand, and caused the seal of the United States to be affixed. Done at the city of Washington, this fifteenth day of June, in the year of our Lord one thousand eight hundred and sixty-three, and of the Independence of the United States the eighty-seventh.

A. LINCOLN.
By the President:
WILLIAM H. SEWARD,
Secretary of State

FACING PAGE: The town of Gettysburg from a broadly northerly direction. Before 1863, Gettysburg was a quiet town with little to suggest it would soon be the scene of a major battle.

juggernaut pressed on to Wrightsville, arriving there the next day. Early had envisioned then threatening Harrisburg from the southwest, but his plan was stymied when he found the bridge over the Susquehanna River to Columbia destroyed. He had little choice but to now return to York and wait for instructions.

In the meantime, Major General Robert Rodes had marched his division from Chambersburg and entered Carlisle on June 27. In a telling show of their presence, the Confederates raised their flag over the U.S. Army cavalry barracks. One brigade commanded by Brigadier General Albert Jenkins continued on toward Harrisburg, camping on a hill 4 miles (6.5 km) outside the capital on the night of June 28. This was the northernmost penetration of the Confederate army for the entire war, but before Jenkins could attack Harrisburg, Lee would issue orders for the Army of Northern Virginia to consolidate. Ewell would soon withdraw and march his corps south to meet the developing situation.

Meade Takes Command

As Lee advanced, Hooker maintained a mixture of uncertainty, lethargy, and frustration. He had started to move slowly after Brandy Station, and by June 19 was spread between Manassas and

Leesburg. There he remained for almost an entire week while Lee moved through Maryland. Hooker did not begin to give chase until June 25 and was not across the Potomac until June 27.

For some time, Hooker had been increasingly feeling that Major General Henry Halleck had been interfering with the Army of the Potomac, and now Hooker had finally had enough. From his headquarters in Frederick, Maryland, he fired off a telegram asking to be relieved. If Hooker had imagined this move as a power play in his quarrel with Halleck, the plan certainly backfired. Lincoln had long since grown frustrated with Hooker and was eager to take this opportunity to replace him with little political repercussion. On June 28, Major General George Meade, former commander of the V Corps, assumed command of the Army of the Potomac. His orders advised him, "Considering the circumstances, no one ever received a more important command."

Indeed, Meade found himself in a most difficult situation. It was not a position he had sought, and he described the order as "totally unexpected." He appeared overwhelmed and intimidated by the responsibility, and wondered, "Why me? Why not Reynolds?"

Part of Meade's apprehension was based on the fact that throughout the Federal march north, he had been kept uninformed by Hooker. Now, upon learning that he was commander of the Army of the Potomac, Meade complained,

ABOVE: Major General Meade was unexpectedly appointed commander of the Army of the Potomac just a few days before the battle at Gettysburg.

"I don't know the Army's position. I don't know its plans. I don't know if it has any plans." Realizing further protest was futile, however, Meade acquiesced, saying, "Well, I've been tried and condemned without a hearing and I suppose I shall have to go to the execution." He acknowledged the order by saying, "As a soldier I obey it, and to the utmost of my ability will execute it." Nonetheless, it was an inauspicious beginning for the fifth commander of the Army of the Potomac, and under such circumstances, Meade would resolve to play it safe.

EXCERPT FROM RODES'S OFFICIAL REPORT OF HIS DIVISION'S ACTIVITY AROUND CARLISLE AND VICINITY

HEADQUARTERS RODES' DIVISION,
Orange Court-House, — —, 1863

Lieut. Col. A. S. PENDLETON
Assistant Adjutant-General, Second Army Corps.

COLONEL:
Resuming its march on the 24th [of June], the division made 14 miles, passing through Chambersburg, which had been reoccupied by General Jenkins that morning, and bivouacked on the Conococheague, 2 miles beyond the town. The Third Alabama Regiment, Colonel Battle commanding, was left in the town as a guard for the people, property, &c. At Chambersburg, the division of General Johnson joined mine, and the two, moving on slowly without noteworthy incident, reached Carlisle on the 27th. The brigades of Daniel, Iverson, and Ramseur occupied the United States barracks at this place, that of General Doles bivouacked on the campus of Dickinson College, a portion of his force acting as guard for the town, while the Alabama brigade bivouacked on and picketed the Baltimore turnpike, 1 mile from town.

Large supplies of cattle, horses, and flour were obtained here and on the march, and in the barracks' stables a large quantity of grain was found. Most of the Government property, excepting the grain, had been removed by the enemy, but musketoons, holsters, tents, and a small quantity of subsistence stores were found in the barracks.

On our arrival at Carlisle, Jenkins' cavalry advanced toward Harrisburg, and had on the 29th made a thorough reconnaissance of the defenses of the place, with a view to our advance upon it, a step which every man in the division contemplated with eagerness, and which was to have been executed on the 30th; but on the 30th, having received orders to move toward the balance of the army, they supposed to be at or near Cashtown, we set out for that place, marching through Petersburg, and bivouacking at Heidlersburg, after a march of at least 22 miles.

I have the honor to be, colonel, yours, very respectfully,

R. E. RODES,
Major General

A Confederate Spy
Meade was not the only commander who suffered from a lack of information. Thanks to Stuart's misguided absence, Lee was also ignorant of the enemy's disposition. What he finally learned of the Federal army came from a mysterious spy named Harrison who reported to James Longstreet. Harrison had left Longstreet at Culpeper and gone to the saloons of Washington where he overheard gossip that Hooker had crossed the Potomac. Traveling at night and learning what he could from soldiers during the day, Harrison made his way to Frederick. There he found two Federal corps. He heard about a third corps nearby, but could not locate it. Having found out that the Army of Northern Virginia was at Chambersburg, Harrison got a horse and headed there. Along the way, he learned two more corps were close to South Mountain. He was also told that Hooker had been replaced by Meade.

On June 28, Harrison reported his findings to Longstreet who sent Major John Fairfax to Lee's headquarters with the news. Personally, Lee had "no confidence in any scout," but without Stuart he was hungry for information. Moreover, Lee knew "General Longstreet thinks a good deal of

LEFT: The remains of the McCormick Barn mark the site of the skirmish at Sporting Hill, fought on June 30.

BELOW: Major General Robert Rodes entered Carlisle with his division on June 27.

Harrison." Lee finally asked for Harrison to come to him and was alarmed by the news. Lee was accustomed to getting such reports from Stuart and now clearly missed this reliable and timely source of intelligence. Regardless of where it came from, however, the news was disturbing. Meade now posed a threat to Lee's communications and initiative. Lee had to concentrate his forces to meet this new development.

Excerpt from Longstreet's Account of His Meeting with Harrison in **From Manassas to Appomattox: Memoirs of the Civil War In America**

After due preparation for our march of the 29th, all hands turned in early for a good night's rest. My mind had hardly turned away from the cares and labors of the day, when I was aroused by some one beating on the pole of my tent. It proved to be Assistant Inspector-

General Fairfax. A young man had been arrested by our outlying pickets under suspicious circumstances. He was looking for General Longstreet's head-quarters, but his comfortable apparel and well-to-do, though travel-stained, appearance caused doubt in the minds of the guards of his being a genuine Confederate who could be trusted about head-quarters. So he was sent up under a file of men to be identified. He proved to be Harrison, the valued scout. He had walked through the lines of the Union army during the night of the 27th and the 28th, secured a mount at dark of the latter day to get in as soon as possible, and brought information of the location of two corps of Federals at night of the 27th, and approximate positions of others. General Hooker had crossed the Potomac on the 25th and 26th of June. On the 27th he had posted two army corps at Frederick, and the scout reported another near them, and two others near South Mountain, as he escaped their lines a little after dark of the 28th. He was sent under care of Colonel Fairfax to make report of his information at general head-quarters. General Lee declined, however, to see him, though he asked Colonel Fairfax as to the information that he brought, and, on hearing it, expressed want of faith in reports of scouts, in which Fairfax generally agreed, but suggested that in this case the information was so near General Longstreet's ideas of the probable movements of the enemy that he gave credit to it. I also sent up a note suggesting a change of direction of the head of our column east. This I thought to be the first and necessary step towards bringing the two armies to such concentration east as would enable us to find a way to draw the enemy into battle, in keeping with the general plan of campaign, and at the same time draw him off from the travel of our trains.

Lee quickly dispatched orders halting Ewell's advance on Harrisburg and Hill's and Longstreet's marches northward. Lee would move his army to the east of South Mountain to compel Meade to follow and so eliminate the threat to the Confederate rear. Still not knowing Stuart's whereabouts, Lee also called in Brigadier General John Imboden's cavalry from its positions guarding the western approaches to the Cumberland Valley. Because it would be at least two days before Imboden could reach Chambersburg, Lee was forced to instruct Longstreet to leave one division behind to protect the trains until Imboden arrived. Longstreet assigned this task to Major General George Pickett. Finally, Lee called in the brigades of Brigadier Generals Beverly Robertson and William Jones from their positions guarding the passes of the Blue Ridge Mountains.

FACING PAGE: Alfred Waud was an illustrator assigned by the *New York Illustrated News* to cover the Army of the Potomac on campaign. This photograph was taken in 1863 sitting in Devil's Den after the Battle of Gettysburg. Many of the sketches in this book were drawn by Waud.

Day One: Confederate Advantage

The first day of the Battle of Gettysburg was a meeting engagement that would be decided largely by which side could get reinforcements in place fastest. The Confederates won this first round of what would become a three-day battle.

By June 30 Lee had gathered most of his army in the area of Chambersburg, Cashtown, and Heidelersburg. In the meantime, Meade was pushing his army north, staying to the east of Lee's army in order to protect Washington, D.C. and Baltimore. "I must move toward the Susquehanna," he explained to Major General Henry Halleck in Washington, "keeping Washington and Baltimore well covered, and if

the enemy is checked in his attempt to cross the Susquehanna, or if he turns toward Baltimore, give him battle."

Meade used march objectives to set a grueling pace for each of his corps. One soldier in Hancock's corps bemoaned a forced march on which he saw men "fall from exhaustion, clothes wet, faces and teeth black with dust, lips parched, eyes sunken, feet blistered, and then driven on at the point of the bayonet." Meade knew what was at stake, and he was well-served by his meticulous chief of staff, Major General

FACING PAGE: General W. S. Hancock is seen directing Major General Doubleday to send his troops to secure Culp's Hill as the embattled Major General Howard looks on. The firm leadership of Winfield Scott Hancock was decisive in restoring order to the Federal line.

RIGHT: Although Daniel Butterfield served well as chief of staff, he had an adversarial relationship with many of his fellow officers after the war, including Meade.

Daniel Butterfield, in keeping the movement under control and on schedule.

Not knowing exactly where Lee's army was, Meade also kept his corps within supporting distance of each other so that no matter which corps struck Lee first, Meade could quickly bring to bear the full weight of his army. He found the seven corps configuration of the army of the Potomac too unwieldy for such vigorous pursuit

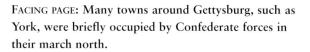

FACING PAGE: **Many towns around Gettysburg, such as York, were briefly occupied by Confederate forces in their march north.**

so he placed Major General John Reynolds in charge of a wing consisting of Reynolds's own I Corps, Major General Dan Sickles's III Corps, Major General Otis Howard's XI Corps, and a cavalry division commanded by Brigadier General John Buford. Behind Reynolds came Major General Henry Slocum's XII Corps and the highly capable Major General Winfield Scott Hancock and his II Corps. Major General George Sykes's V Corps and Major General John Sedgwick's large VI Corps guarded the army's east flank.

Rookie Commanders

Meade was not the only man new to his job in the Army of the Potomac. Of these seven corps, not one was now led by the same officer who had led it at the Battle of Antietam (September 17, 1862). Of the 19 infantry divisions, all but three had also changed command since then. Brigades were supposed to be commanded by brigadier generals, but fewer than half of the 51 brigades were led by an officer of that rank. Perhaps as important, only 10 of the 51 had a commander who had led the brigade for at least 10 months. The situation at the regimental level was even worse. As Bruce Catton described it, the Army of the Potomac was "an army in which the whole problem of command had gone unsolved."

BELOW: **This magazine illustration shows Meade and his staff discussing strategy. Meade conducted several councils of war during the Gettysburg Campaign.**

Under these less than ideal circumstances, Meade pressed on, hoping to catch Lee and force him to turn and fight. By the end of June 29, the Army of the Potomac had covered 25 miles (40 km) and was spread out along a 20-mile (32 km) front near the Pennsylvania border stretching from Emmitsburg southeast to Westminster, Maryland.

The next day, Meade advised Reynolds that reports of Lee's current dispositions and the

LEFT: Divisional commander Henry Heth was one of the more popular officers in the Army of Northern Virginia and said to be the only one that Lee called by his first name.

EXCERPT FROM LETTER OF LIEUTENANT COLONEL RUFUS DAWES, AN OFFICER IN THE 6TH WISCONSIN VOLUNTEERS, TO M. G. B.

Bivouac near Middleton, MD
June 27, 1863

We left our camp near Guilford station on Broad Run, early on the morning of the twenty fifth. We marched all night and crossed the Potomac at Edwards Ferry. We proceeded via Poolsville and encamped for the night near Barnesville. We marched next morning at daylight . . . through deep mud and a drizzling rain all day and encamped near Jefferson in the valley of Middleton. This morning we started early and reached this point at two o'clock. Our marches have been long and toilsome. What do you think of trudging along all day in a soaking rain, getting as wet as a drowned rat, taking supper on hard tack and salt pork, and then wrapping up in a wet woolen blanket and lying down for a sleep, but waked up during the night three or four times to receive and attend to orders and finally turning out at three o'clock in the morning to get the regiment ready to march? Well, that is soldiering and it is a great deal more comfortable soldiering than to march through suffocating clouds of dust under a hot sun. In the dust men are dogged and silent. In the rain they are often even hilarious and jolly.

Rufus Dawes

existing road network suggested Lee would concentrate his forces near the small town of Gettysburg, Pennsylvania. All told, 10 roads led to Gettysburg from Chambersburg, Mummasburg, Carlisle, Harrisburg, York, Hanover, Baltimore, Taneytown, Emmitsburg, and Hagerstown. Reynolds thus sent Buford and two cavalry brigades toward Gettysburg to find Lee.

The Quest for Shoes

While Buford was scouting toward Gettysburg, he encountered the brigade of Brigadier General James Pettigrew who had marched to Gettysburg that morning to secure some shoes reported to be in the town. Upon his arrival, Pettigrew saw no enemy in Gettysburg, but did observe the long column of Federal troops advancing from Emmitsburg. Not wanting to bring on a general engagement without orders, Pettigrew withdrew to Cashtown and reported his observations to his division commander, Major General Henry Heth. While the two men were talking, Ambrose Powell Hill rode up and joined the discussion.

RIGHT: Shoes were a valuable commodity to Civil War soldiers such as these Confederates preparing to cross the Potomac River.

Hill stated that the Federal cavalry was probably just an outpost, and that "the enemy are still at Middleburg, and have not yet struck their tents." Heth agreed and asked permission to return to Gettysburg the next day to "search the town for army supplies (shoes especially) and return the next day." Hill authorized the mission, and thus began the popular tale that the most famous battle of the Civil War was fought over shoes.

In spite of this oversimplification, the importance of shoes to Lee's army was very real. The Confederacy's weak industrial and manufacturing base created numerous supply shortages, but, according to American Historian Bell Irvin Wiley (1906–1980), "the most pervasive and the most keenly felt of all deficiencies was that of shoes." "The Rebel Army was a walking army," Wiley explains, and "the expenditure of leather entailed by these arduous marches was tremendous." Certainly if Heth thought there was a stockpile of shoes nearby, he would go looking for it.

The evidence seems to suggest, however, that Heth was destined to be disappointed. Although Jubal Early had requisitioned shoes at Gettysburg on June 26, he certainly did not report the presence of any shoe factory that had somehow been rumored to exist. Indeed, the 1860 U.S. Census listed 22 shoemakers in Gettysburg, but neither a shoe factory nor a shoe warehouse.

BELOW: Today roads, such as this one over Willoughby Run, crisscross the old Gettysburg battlefield. Willoughby Run was the scene of early skirmishes between the two armies.

Nonetheless the Confederate quest for shoes has become enshrined as the proximate cause of the great battle about to be fought at Gettysburg. In the prose of Shelby Foote, "That was how they came, three-deep and booming; Heth was on his way to 'get those shoes.'"

In the meantime, Buford had recognized the value of Gettysburg not as a source of shoes but as a road junction, and he organized his small force to defend it. To the west of town was a series of generally north-south running ridges. The furthest west and the most pronounced was Herr's Ridge, about 1.5 miles (2.5 km) from Gettysburg. A tavern located on its crest gave the ridge its name. About 900 yards (825 m) to the east was McPherson's Ridge, named after the family that farmed there. Between these two ridges was low ground through which meandered a small stream called Willoughby Run. Chambersburg Pike led into Gettysburg from the northwest passed the McPhersons' farm. Running parallel to the pike some 200 yards (180 m) to the north was a railbed, but no track had been laid on it.

Continuing east another 500 yards (450 m), to a point about three quarters of a mile (1.2 km) from Gettysburg, lay the well-wooded Seminary Ridge and its Lutheran Theological Seminary. A little north of Chambersburg Pike, Seminary Ridge merged with the generally open and rolling McPherson's Ridge. At that junction, Oak Ridge ran northward to the 80-foot (25 m) high Oak Knob that dominated the northwest side of Gettysburg.

Buford positioned his brigades in depth in dismounted positions along this series of ridges

FACING PAGE: General John Buford sits astride his horse beside the McPherson barn and directs Calef's battery into position. The Union troops at McPherson's Ridge held their line against the advancing Confederates until re-enforcements arrived.

EXCERPT FROM BUFORD'S OFFICIAL REPORT OF HIS DIVISION'S ACTIONS ON JULY 1

HEADQUARTERS FIRST CAVALRY DIVISION
August 27, 1863
Lieut. Col. C. Ross SMITH,
Chief of Staff, Cavalry Corps.

Colonel:
By daylight on July 1, I had gained positive information of the enemy's position and movements, and my arrangements were made for entertaining him until General Reynolds could reach the scene.

On July 1, between 8 and 9 a.m., reports came in from the First Brigade (Colonel Gamble's) that the enemy was coming down from toward Cashtown in force. Colonel Gamble made an admirable line of battle, and moved off proudly to meet him. The two lines soon became hotly engaged, we having the advantage of position, he of numbers. The First Brigade held its own for more than two hours, and had to be literally dragged back a few hundred yards to a position more secure and better sheltered. Tidball's battery, commanded by Lieutenant Calef, Second U.S. Artillery, fought on this occasion as is seldom witnessed. At one time the enemy had a concentric fire upon this battery from twelve guns, all at short range. Calef held his own gloriously, worked his guns deliberately with great judgment and skill, and with wonderful effect upon the enemy. The First Brigade

maintained this unequal contest until the leading division of General Reynolds' corps came up to its assistance, and then most reluctantly did it give up the front. A portion of the Third Indiana found horse-holders, borrowed muskets, and fought with the Wisconsin regiment that came to relieve them. While this left of my line was engaged, Devin's brigade, on the right, had its hands full. The enemy advanced upon Devin by four roads, and on each was checked and held until the leading division of the Eleventh Corps came to his relief. . . .

The zeal, bravery, and good behavior of the officers and men on the night of June 30, and during July 1, was commendable in the extreme. A heavy task was before us; we were equal to it, and shall all remember with pride that at Gettysburg we did our country much service.

I am, very respectfully, your obedient servant,

JNO. BUFORD,
Brigadier General of Volunteers,
Commanding

RIGHT: Buford's monument at Gettysburg reads: "From this crest was fired the opening gun of the battle: one of the four cannon at the base of this memorial."

ABOVE: At the time of the battle, the railroad (shown here) that ran parallel to Chambersburg Pike was unfinished.

force represented two-thirds of Hill's corps, but Hill, who did not feel well, remained at Cashtown. He would play little part in the unfolding action, leaving matters to Heth who was the least experienced division commander in the corps. Lee, desirous of first concentrating his army, had instructed Heth on June 30 not to bring on a general engagement.

First Contact

The order of the Confederate march was the brigades of Brigadier Generals James Archer, Joseph Davis, James Pettigrew, and John Brockenbrough. Heth expected to meet little resistance, but at 7:30 a.m., Lieutenant John Calef, commanding the six guns of Battery A, 2nd U.S. Artillery, opened fire at a range of about three quarters of a mile (1.2 km). Soon Confederate and Federal pickets were exchanging shots. When he encountered Buford's dismounted cavalry on McPherson's Ridge, Heth deployed Archer's and Davis's brigades on line "to move forward and occupy the town," expecting to push quickly through what he thought was only a small Federal reconnaissance force. Such an act was clearly not within the intent of Lee's orders not to bring on a general engagement.

Archer moved eastward down the Chambersburg road until he began receiving fire from Calef's guns. Archer formed three skirmish lines and returned fire with his own artillery. By then, Heth had come forward to assess the situation. He ordered Davis to come on line to

and posted advanced pickets in a wide arc from the Hagerstown road in the southwest to the Harrisburg road in the northeast. His pickets on Chambersburg Pike could already see Confederate campfires in the distance, and he cautioned one of his brigade commanders that

the enemy "will attack in the morning and they will come booming—skirmishers three deep. You will have to fight like the devil until support arrives." Buford's orders from his cavalry corps commander, Major General Pleasonton, had been to "cover and protect the front." He intended to do so.

Buford was right. At about 5:00 a.m. on July 1, Heth left Cashtown with two divisions supported by two battalions of artillery. The

Archer's left and for the two brigades to move forward together.

Contrary to Heth's prediction, Buford resisted vigorously with Colonel William Gamble's dismounted men holding positions along the east bank of Willoughby Run in a 1,000-yard (900 m) line from the railbed across the Chambersburg Pike and Colonel Thomas Devin's brigade north of the railbed to the base of Oak Hill. The stubborn Federal resistance halted the Confederate advance, but Buford had just 2,748 men opposing Heth's 7,461. Moreover, part of the Federal force had to be detailed to hold horses. Buford quickly requested reinforcements from Reynolds. Additional Confederate forces were also on their way. Indeed, in large part, this opening encounter of the Battle of Gettysburg would be decided by which side could most quickly respond to the unexpected contact and get troops to the decisive point.

McPherson's Ridge

Reynolds had gone to bed on June 30 without orders for the next day. When orders finally arrived at 4:00 a.m. on July 1, he wasted no time. Brigadier General James Wadsworth's division had led the previous day's march, and Reynolds left Wadsworth in the van to expedite matters. Major General Abner Doubleday would follow with the rest of I Corps, allowing

FACING PAGE: Battlefield visitors observe the general area where Reynolds was killed.

Reynolds to focus on the entire wing. Howard's XI Corps would be next and then Sickles and his III Corps. Wadsworth was moving along the Emmitsburg Road by 8:00 a.m. with Reynolds traveling up front with him. Still Reynolds had little information about what lay ahead of him.

As Reynolds advanced, he was met by a courier from Buford telling him that the

BELOW: Titled "For God's Sake Forward," this painting by Don Troiani shows the men of the 2nd Wisconsin (Iron Brigade), lead by General John F. Reynolds, rush into a grove of trees on McPherson's Ridge to meet the Confederate advance.

ABOVE: Men of Archer's 1st Tennessee withdraw following the fight with the Iron Brigade on McPherson's Ridge. William Murray of the 19th Indiana reported: "The Tennessee color bearer broke through the lines and run up a slope, and then turned and shook the flag at our troops and disappeared from sight."

Confederates were marching down the Chambersburg Pike toward Gettysburg. Reynolds hurried forward and found Buford who greeted him with the sober report that "The devil's to pay." Together, the men observed the developing situation from the cupola of the three-story Lutheran Theological Seminary on the western edge of town. It was about 9:00 a.m. and Gamble's men were beginning to be pushed back across Willoughby Run. Reynolds asked Buford if he thought he could hold on with his cavalry until the I Corps could arrive, and Buford said he thought he could.

Reynolds was a proven professional and a hard fighter with a reputation as a "soldier general." He was also a Pennsylvanian bent on expelling an enemy from his state. He sent word to Meade that "The enemy is advancing in a strong force, and I fear they will get to the heights beyond the town before I can. I will fight them inch by inch, and if driven into the town I will barricade the streets and hold them back as long as possible." When Meade got the report he said, "Good! That is just like Reynolds. He will hold out to the bitter end."

At 10:00 a.m. Wadsworth arrived at McPherson's Ridge with his division. He threw Brigadier General Lysander Cutler's brigade into action with Brigadier General Solomon Meredith's Iron Brigade close on their heels. Heth sent Davis and Archer forward in force on either side of the pike. When Archer's men realized they were up against "those damned black-hatted fellows," they knew they were in

FACING PAGE: The 24th Regiment Michigan Volunteers fought a desperate rear guard action near the Lutheran Seminary at Gettysburg. The 24th Michigan suffered 80 percent casualties in the fighting.

for a fight. By now, both sides had realized that the 5-acre (2 hectares) McPherson's Woods was the key to the ridge. Archer proceeded cautiously, but Heth urged him forward. At the same time, Reynolds ordered, "Forward men, forward for God's sake and drive those fellows out of those woods."

Archer's and Meredith's men collided at the crest of the ridge. Buford's men then withdrew behind the infantry, and the Federals enjoyed early success. Archer was forced back and after an hour of fighting had lost about a third of his force. As his men retreated, they found their way blocked by a high fence, and about 75 were captured while they waited for their turn to climb over. To his great embarrassment, Archer was among those captured. He was brought to Doubleday, an old army acquaintance. "Good morning, Archer!" said Doubleday with an outstretched hand. "How are you? I am glad to see you." Ignoring Doubleday's gesture Archer sniffed, "Well, I am not glad to see you by a damn sight!"

Not all the news was so good for the Federals. As the 2nd Wisconsin of Meredith's brigade had passed by him, Reynolds had turned to check on the advance of the attack. As he did, a bullet struck him in the back of the neck, killing him instantly. With the loss of

EXCERPT FROM HETH'S OFFICIAL REPORT OF HIS DIVISION'S ACTION ON JULY 1

HEADQUARTERS HETH'S DIVISION
Camp near Orange Court-House,
September 13, 1863

Capt. W. N. STARKE,
Asst. Adjt. Gen., Third Corps, Army of Northern Virginia

CAPTAIN: I have the honor to report the operations of my division from June 29 until July 1, including the part it took in the battle of Gettysburg (first day), July 1.

The division reached Cashtown, Pa., on June 29. Cashtown is situated at the base of the South Mountain, on the direct road from Chambersburg, via Fayetteville, to Gettysburg, and 9 miles distant from the latter place.

On the morning of June 30, I ordered Brigadier-General Pettigrew to take his brigade to Gettysburg, search the town for army supplies (shoes especially), and return the same day. On reaching the suburbs of Gettysburg, General Pettigrew found a large force of cavalry near the town, supported by an infantry force. Under these circumstances, he did not deem it advisable to enter the town, and returned, as directed, to Cashtown. The result of General Pettigrew's observations was reported to Lieutenant-General Hill, who reached Cashtown on the evening of the 30th.

On July 1, my division, accompanied by Pegram's battalion of artillery, was ordered to move at 5 a.m. in the direction of Gettysburg. On nearing Gettysburg, it was evident that the enemy was in the vicinity of the town in some force.

It may not be improper to remark that at this time—9 o'clock on the morning of July 1—I was ignorant what force was at or near Gettysburg, and supposed it consisted of cavalry, most probably supported by a brigade or two of infantry.

On reaching the summit of the second ridge of hills west of Gettysburg, it became evident that there were infantry, cavalry, and artillery in and around the town. A few shots from Pegram's battalion (Marye's battery) scattered the cavalry vedettes. One of the first shells fired by Pegram mortally wounded Major-General Reynolds, then in command of the force at Gettysburg.

I am, very respectfully, your obedient servant,

H. HETH,
Major General

Reynolds, Doubleday assumed command of the battlefield.

In the Thick of Battle

While the Iron Brigade was consolidating its gains south of the Chambersburg Pike, the situation on the north side was quite the opposite. There, Davis's Mississippians had advanced on a half mile-wide (0.8 km) front using the unfinished railroad bed that paralleled the pike as cover. When they attacked across the crest of McPherson's Ridge, the Confederates caught Cutler's brigade by surprise. As Davis described it, "The engagement soon became very warm."

The Confederates caught the approaching Federals as they tried to deploy from column into line formation. As Davis pressed his advantage, Wadsworth ordered a retreat. By this time, however, two of Davis's regimental commanders had become casualties, and he was beginning to lose control of the attack. Although Cutler's men were falling back toward Seminary Ridge, Davis found himself struggling to manage a brigade "jumbled together without regard to regiment or company."

When Doubleday ordered the 6th Wisconsin, a regiment he had held in reserve, forward, the Mississippians were unable to respond. Davis withdrew his shattered command to Herr's Ridge, but not before some 232 of his men had been captured. It was a costly victory for the 6th Wisconsin, however.

Nearly 200 of its 420 members became casualties in the attack.

As both sides struggled to assess the confusing situation, somewhat of a lull descended on the battlefield at around 11:00 a.m. For the next two hours or so, actual fighting remained relatively quiet as reinforcements flowed in and commanders hurried them into position. Sometime during this interval, John Burns, a 69-year-old constable and variously reported veteran of the War of 1812, the Seminole Wars, and the Mexican-American War, calmly strode up to the battlefield. Carrying a flintlock musket, Burns found an officer of the

ABOVE: Reynolds's monument at Gettysburg follows the perhaps coincidental rule that a horse with two feet off the ground indicates its rider was killed in battle.

LEFT: The fighting between the Iron Brigade and the 2nd Mississippi was among the fiercest at Gettysburg.

Pennsylvania 155th "Bucktail" Regiment and requested to join the ranks. The surprised officer sent Burns into the woods next to the McPherson Farm, where he fought beside members of the Iron Brigade throughout the afternoon.

Burns suffered three wounds throughout the fighting. He was captured by the Confederates, but released a short time later. Known as "The Old Hero of Gettysburg," Burns soon won national acclaim. In fact, President Lincoln praised Burns as the first resident he wished to meet when he traveled to Gettysburg to dedicate the Soldiers' National Cemetery there in November.

Excerpt From "John Burns of Gettysburg," A Poem by Francis Bret Harte

Have you heard of a story that gossips tell
Of Burns of Gettysburg? No? Ah, well:
Brief is the glory that hero earns,
Briefer the story of poor John Burns:
He was the fellow who won reknown,
The only man who didn't back down
When the rebels rode through his native town;
But held his own in the fight next day,

When all his townsfolk ran away....
So raged the battle. You know the rest:
How the rebels, beaten and backward pressed,
Broke at the final charge and ran.
At which John Burns—a practical man—
Shouldered his rifle, unbent his brows,
And then went back to his bees and cows.
That is the story of old John Burns;
This is the moral the reader learns:
In fighting the battle, the question's whether
You'll show a hat that's white or a feather.

Part of the reason for the loss of momentum on the Federal side had been the death of Reynolds. However, when Howard arrived with his XI Corps and assumed command, the Federals rallied. Confederate troops were also rushing to the sound of the guns, and Ewell had his corps moving south from Carlisle and Heidlersburg to the action. Howard sent a desperate request to Sickles and Slocum to bring their corps forward. "General Reynolds is killed," wrote Howard urgently. "For God's sake, come up."

Howard had earlier observed the importance of Cemetery Hill on the north end of Cemetery Ridge. The hill dominated the approaches to Gettysburg and would be key to any defensive effort. He dispatched Brigadier General Adolph von Steinwehr's division to occupy the position, giving them orders to hold their ground "at all hazards."

Heavily Engaged

The Federal high command was not alone in its confusion. Hearing the fighting in the distance, Lee had rode forward and found the ailing Hill who could provide little in the way of information. Still from the mere sound of the battle, Lee knew his cautions against bringing on a general engagement had been ignored. Moreover, he now had infantry stumbling forward across unfamiliar terrain doing a task for which cavalry was better suited. "I cannot think what has become of Stuart," Lee told Brigadier General Richard Anderson. "I ought to have heard from him long before now. He may have met with disaster, but I hope not." The problem for Lee was that "In the absence of reports from him, I am in ignorance of what we have in front of us here. It may be the whole Federal army, or it may be only a detachment. If it is the whole Federal force, we must fight a battle here." Amid this uncertainty, Lee continued forward.

At about 2:30 p.m., Lee ascended Herr's Ridge where he could get a view of the battlefield. Heth soon found Lee and

BELOW: Rodes's division advanced up Oak Ridge, shown here in a circa 1900 photograph.

reported, "Rodes is heavily engaged. Had I not better attack?" Still concerned that he did not completely understand the situation, Lee said, "No, I am not prepared to bring on a general engagement today. Longstreet is not up." Lee's opinion soon changed when he saw what was developing on the northern flank of the Federal line.

There, Rodes's Division from Ewell's Corps was moving up Oak Ridge and Major General Jubal Early's Division was advancing to the east along the line of the road to Harrisburg. One of Rodes's brigades found a quarter-mile gap (0.4 km) between the two Federal corps. As Rodes said later, as far as he could see, the enemy "had no troops facing me at all." Rodes posted his artillery battalion commanded by Lieutenant Colonel Thomas Carter on Oak Hill to suppress the Federals while Rodes deployed his infantry. When Carter fired into the Federal flank, he drew a surprisingly quick response from Brigadier General Henry Baxter's brigade of Brigadier General John Robinson's I Corps division. These Federals had only recently occupied a hasty position behind a stone wall along a stretch of the Mummasburg road that faced generally north. Baxter's 1,400 men were trying to buy time for the XI Corps elements then hurrying forward from Gettysburg. Rodes knew his opportunity was a fleeting one, and he

FACING PAGE: Barlow's Knoll shortly after the battle. In occupying the small rise that came to bear his name, Barlow created a salient in the XI Corps line.

BELOW: Although a lawyer by trade, John Gordon proved a capable general.

pushed forward without additional reconnaissance or skirmishers.

In his haste to attack, Rodes ended up sending his brigades piecemeal into the action, and Baxter's men fought back hard. It looked as if both sides were about spent when Early's division joined the battle. This arrival of fresh Confederate troops put added pressure on what was already a defense under stress.

The long, thin Federal line was bent at a right angle with XI Corps stretching from east to west and I Corps from north to south. While Rodes was hammering the vertex of the angle, Early was now descending upon the Federal right. If Hill could be brought to bear on the Federal left, Lee thought, the enemy would be crushed in between. He ordered Heth and Major General William Pender forward to exploit the opportunity.

On the far right of Howard's XI Corps, Brigadier General Francis Barlow anchored his flank on a small rise that later became known as Barlow's Knoll. To occupy that location, Barlow had moved well ahead of Brigadier General Alexander Schimmelfennig's division. As Major General Carl Schurz, temporarily commanding Howard's Corps, ordered Schimmelfennig forward to correct the alignment, fighting began in earnest. Brigadier General John Gordon smashed into

Barlow's front while brigades commanded by Brigadier General Harry Hays and Colonel Isaac Avery attacked on both sides of the Heidlersburg road and turned Barlow's right flank. Barlow's men panicked and beat a hasty retreat to Gettysburg. Barlow was wounded in the rout, and the collapse of his division was followed by failures throughout the XI Corps line. Barlow was left for dead when Gordon happened upon him. At Barlow's request, Gordon scribbled a note to Mrs. Barlow telling her that her husband's dying thoughts were of her. Gordon then carried Barlow to the shade of a tree and rejoined the battle. Remarkably, Barlow would survive, but the collapse of his and Schimmelfennig's divisions left the I Corps' position on Seminary Ridge in great danger.

Withdrawal to Seminary Ridge

Moments after Lee had given the order, Heth had advanced down Herr's Ridge toward Doubleday's I Corps. Heth had Colonel John Brockenbrough's brigade on the left, Brigadier General James Pettigrew's brigade in the center, and Archer's brigade, now led by Colonel Birkett Fry on the right. Davis's brigade had suffered too many casualties already and remained in the rear. Just after the attack crossed Willoughby Run, Heth was seriously wounded by a Minie ball and Pettigrew assumed command of the division.

FACING PAGE: A mounted Gordon leads his brigade forward at Gettysburg.

FACING PAGE: Cemetery Hill dominated the approaches to Gettysburg and became the Federal rallying point and position for much of the Federal artillery.

The fighting was ferocious and both sides took terrible casualties, but eventually the Confederates got around the I Corps' left flank and Federals fell back to Seminary Ridge. There the Federals reformed behind some crude breastworks, but soon Pender's division was upon them. Before long, the I Corps' line was broken. Howard's foresight in securing Cemetery Hill earlier now proved particularly fortuitous for the Federals, and the blue wave headed for the safety of a new defensive line built around Steinwehr's position there.

Culp's Hill and Cemetery Hill

At first the movement was orderly, but as the Federals surged through Gettysburg, the retreat became a little more rapid. Upon arriving at Steinwehr's position, however, the Federals regained their composure, and when II Corps commander Major General Winfield Scott Hancock arrived on the scene to take charge of the sector, order was restored. Due east of Cemetery Hill, Hancock saw a saddle that ran half a mile (0.8 km) to another high point called Culp's Hill. Confederate patrols were already moving toward a ravine that cut into the saddle from the north, halfway between the two hills. He knew if the Confederates got control of Culp's Hill, the Federal line would be compromised. As Doubleday was collecting the

EXCERPT FROM GORDON'S OFFICIAL REPORT OF HIS BRIGADE'S ACTIONS ON JULY 1

August 10, 1863
Maj. JOHN W. DANIEL,
Assistant Adjutant-General, Early's Division

MAJOR:
Marching thence to Gettysburg, we participated in the battle of July 1. In accordance with orders from Major-General Early, I formed my brigade in line of battle on the right of the division, one regiment (the 26th Georgia) having been detached to support the artillery under Lt-Colonel Jones.

About 3 p.m. I was ordered to move my brigade forward to the support of Major-General Rodes' left. The men were much fatigued from long marches, and I therefore caused them to move forward slowly until within about 300 yards of the enemy's line, when the advance was as rapid as the nature of the ground and a proper regard for the preservation of my line would permit. The enemy had succeeded in gaining a position upon the left flank of Doles' brigade, and in causing these troops to retreat. This movement of the enemy would necessarily have exposed his right flank but for the precaution he had taken to cover it by another line. It was upon this line ... that my brigade charged. Moving forward under heavy fire over rail and plank fences, and crossing a creek whose banks were so abrupt as to prevent a passage excepting at certain points, this brigade rushed upon the enemy with a resolution and spirit, in my opinion, rarely excelled. The enemy

made a most obstinate resistance until the colors on portions of the two lines were separated by a space of less than 50 paces, when his line was broken and driven back, leaving the flank which this line had protected exposed to the fire from my brigade. An effort was here made by the enemy to change his front and check our advance, but the effort failed, and this line, too, was driven back in the greatest confusion, and with immense loss in killed, wounded, and prisoners. Among the latter was a division commander (General [F. C.] Barlow), who was severely wounded. I was here ordered by Major-General Early to halt.

I had no means of ascertaining the number of the enemy's wounded by the fire of this brigade, but if these were in the usual proportion to his killed, nearly 300 of whom were buried on the ground where my brigade fought, his loss in killed and wounded must have exceeded the number of men I carried into action. Neither was it possible for me to take any account of the prisoners sent to the rear, but the division inspector credits this brigade with about 1,800. ...

The loss of the brigade in killed and wounded was 350, of whom 40 were killed.

I am, major, very respectfully, your obedient servant,

J. B. GORDON,
Brigadier General

LEFT: Culp's Hill formed the tip of what would become the fishhooked-shaped Federal line.

FACING PAGE: Sharpshooters occupied houses in the town of Gettysburg, as the fighting soon spread there.

BELOW: Winfield Scott Hancock received the "Thanks of Congress" for his actions at Gettysburg.

remnants of I Corps, Hancock told him to send a division to occupy Culp's Hill. At first Doubleday protested, but Hancock insisted. "Sir," he said. "I am commander on this field. Send every man you have got!" With that, Doubleday ordered Wadsworth's division to Culp's Hill.

With the Federal position now extended from Cemetery Hill east to Culp's Hill, Hancock then reconnoitered the area with Slocum and Major General Gouverneur Warren, Meade's chief engineer. Meade had earlier asked Hancock for his recommendation as to whether or not Gettysburg would be a good place to fight. Hancock now said that it was an advantageous position for a general engagement, a conclusion with which Meade concurred. In fact, he had already begun moving his army there.

As the defeated XI Corps withdrew to the safety of Cemetery Hill, they passed

Entrance to Gettysburg — Sharpshooting from the houses —

through Gettysburg's narrow streets. Hays's and Avery's brigades were in hot pursuit, and the sight of the retreating Federals and victorious Confederates threw the townspeople into a panic. Liberty Hollinger recalled, "We watched through the cellar windows, and, Oh, what horror filled our breasts as we gazed upon their bayonets and heard the deafening roar of musketry. Yes, we were really in the midst of an awful reality." Soon the 1st South Carolina raised its flag in Gettysburg's town square.

Around 5:00 p.m., Ewell rode into Gettysburg and began to take stock of the situation. With Early he rode out Baltimore Street to survey the gathering Federal force on Cemetery Hill and saw batteries of artillery supported by lines of infantry. It was an imposing sight, and while Ewell was still processing it, orders arrived from Lee. Ewell was "to carry the hill occupied by the enemy [Cemetery Hill], if he found it practicable, but to avoid a general engagement until the arrival of the other divisions of the army."

It was the type of discretionary order that Stonewall Jackson would have energetically executed, but Ewell, new to corps command, hesitated. As Ewell waited for the arrival of Edward Johnson's division, the Federals strengthened their defense. By the time Johnson

FACING PAGE: Conferate infantry man a barricade during the brief fighting for the town of Gettysburg before Federal forces withdrew to Culp's Hill and Cemetery Hill to the south.

arrived, it was too late to attack. Ewell ordered his corps to rest for the night.

Entry From Sarah Broadhead's Diary, July 1

I got up early this morning to get my baking done before any fighting would begin. I had just put my bread in the pans when the cannons began to fire, and true enough the battle had begun in earnest, about two miles out on the Chambersburg pike. What to do or where to go, I did not know. People were running here and there, screaming that the town would be shelled. No one knew where to go or what to do. My husband advised remaining where we were, but all said we ought not to remain in

EXCERPT FROM COLONEL WILLIAM ROBINSON'S OFFICIAL REPORT OF HIS REGIMENT'S ACTIONS ON JULY 1

HEADQUARTERS SEVENTH WISCONSIN VOLUNTEERS
November 18, 1863

Capt. J. D. WOOD,
Assistant Adjutant-General, First Brigade

Sir:
... During this movement we were exposed not only to the fire of the advancing enemy in front, but also to that from the brigade which had turned our left flank, and was now advancing from that direction in line obliquely to our new position. It was with some difficulty I restrained the men from firing until the enemy got as near as I wanted them. When they were within easy range, the order was given, and their ranks went down like grass before the scythe from the united fire of our regiments and the battery. There were very few, if any, of that brigade escaped death or wounds. The regiment held this position until all the troops on our right and left had retired. The battery had limbered up and retired. The enemy, in overwhelming numbers, had again turned both our flanks, with a line formed on each perpendicular to ours, and reaching a considerable distance to our rear, forming three sides of a square around us, with the open side to our rear and toward the town.

At this time Captain Richardson, of the brigade staff, again brought me the order to retire through the town. I again retired, by the right of companies to the rear, through the orchard over the ridge, and then by the right flank by file left into column, and moved on to the turnpike and through the town to Cemetery Hill, being the rear of the troops from that part of the field.

Respectfully, your obedient servant,

W. W. ROBINSON,
Colonel, Seventh Wisconsin Volunteers

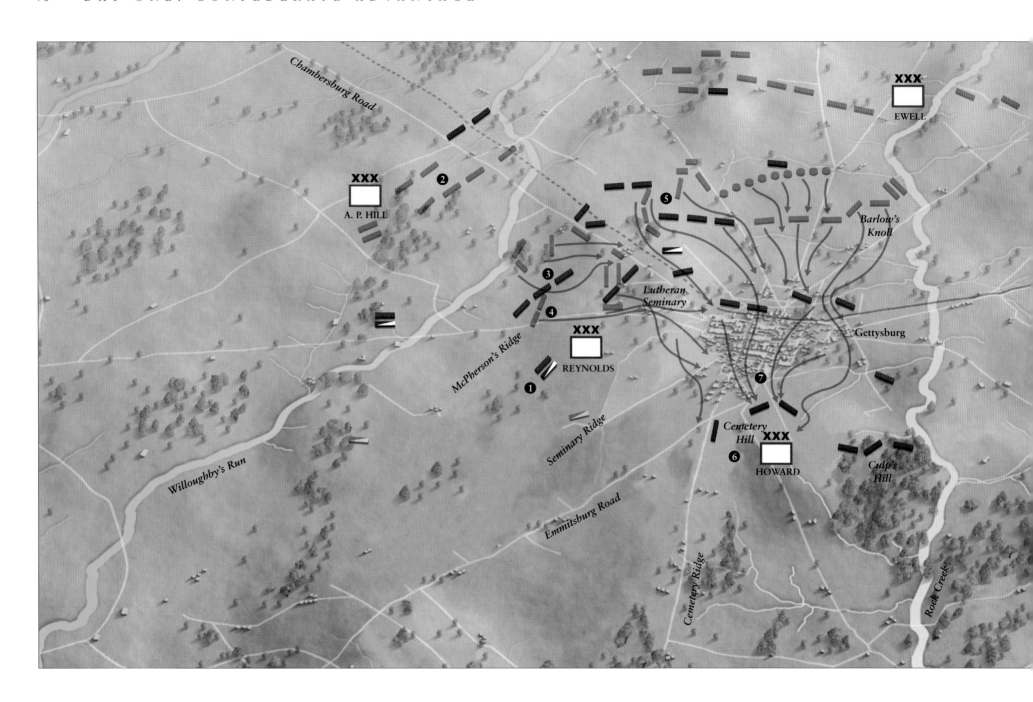

Baltimore Road

PHASE ONE
July 1

❶ At 4:00 a.m. on July 1, Reynolds received orders to move his corps toward Gettysburg. Buford's cavalry was already manning a thin line west of the town.

❷ At about 5:00 a.m., Heth's division (part of A. P. Hill's Corps) left Cashtown for Gettysburg with instructions not to bring on a general engagement.

❸ At about 7:30 a.m., the first shots were exchanged between Buford and Heth, and a meeting engagement soon developed.

❹ At 10:00 a.m., Wadsworth's division, the lead unit on Reynolds's march, arrived at McPherson's Ridge. Reynolds was killed hurrying reinforcements forward.

❺ At about 3:00 p.m., first Rodes and then Early launched an attack that forced Howard to retreat.

❻ The retreating Federals fell back through Gettysburg to Cemetery Hill, where Howard had earlier ordered von Steinwehr to establish a position.

❼ At about 5:00 p.m., Ewell entered Gettysburg. Lee ordered him to seize Cemetery Hill "if practicable," but Ewell did not attack.

our exposed position, and that it would be better to go to some part of the town farther away from the scene of the conflict. As our neighbors had all gone away, I would not remain, but my husband said he would stay at home. About 10 o'clock the shells began to "fly around quite thick," and I took my child and went to the house of a friend up town.

As we passed up the street we met wounded men coming in from the field. When we saw them, we, for the first time, began to realize our fearful situation, and anxiously to ask, Will our army be whipped? Some said there was no danger of that yet, and pointed to Confederate prisoners who began to be sent through our streets to the rear. Such a dirty, filthy set, no one ever saw. They were dressed in all kinds of clothes, of all kinds and no kind of cuts. Some were barefooted and a few wounded. Though enemies, I pitied them. I, with others, was sitting at the doorstep bathing the wounds of some of our brave soldiers, and became so much excited as the artillery galloped through the town, and the infantry hurried out to reinforce those fighting, that for a time we forgot our fears and our danger.

All was bustle and confusion. No one can imagine in what extreme fright we were when our men began to retreat. A citizen galloped up to the door in which we were sitting and called out, "For God's sake go in the house! The Rebels are in the other end of town, and all will be killed!" We quickly ran in, and the cannonading coming nearer and becoming

heavier, we went to the cellar, and in a few minutes the town was full of the filthy Rebels. They did not get farther, for our soldiers having possession of the hills just beyond, shelled them so that they were glad to give over the pursuit, and the fighting for the day was ended.

We remained in the cellar until the firing ceased, and then feared to come out, not knowing what the Rebels might do. How changed the town looked when we came to the light. The street was strewn over with clothes, blankets, knapsacks, cartridge-boxes, dead horses, and the bodies of a few men, but not so many of these last as I expected to see. "Can we go out?" was asked of the Rebels. "Certainly," was the answer; "they would not hurt us." We started hoe, and found things all right. As I write all is quiet, but O! how I dread to-morrow.

Heavy Losses

The Federal army was badly bruised in the first day's fighting. The I Corps had started the day with some 10,000 men in action and was now down to perhaps 2,400. The Iron Brigade lost almost two-thirds of its 1,800 fighting force. The 24th Michigan, the largest regiment in the brigade, lost 399 of its 496 men for a total of 80 percent casualties.

The XI Corps did not suffer as many killed or wounded, but nearly 4,000 of its men had been captured and another 1,500, who would later be

LEFT: The bodies of Confederate soldiers are collected near McPherson's woods following the first day's fighting.

EXCERPT FROM EWELL'S OFFICIAL REPORT EXPLAINING HIS DECISION NOT TO ATTACK CEMETERY HILL

HDQRS. SECOND CORPS, ARMY OF NORTHERN VIRGINIA
-------- ---, 1863.
Col. R. H. CHILTON,
Assistant Adjutant and Inspector General

COLONEL:
The enemy had fallen back to a commanding position known as Cemetery Hill, south of Gettysburg, and quickly showed a formidable front there. On entering the town, I received a message from the commanding general to attack this hill, if I could do so to advantage. I could not bring artillery to bear on it, and all the troops with me were jaded by twelve hours' marching and fighting, and I was notified that General Johnson's division (the only one of my corps that had not been engaged) was close to the town.

Cemetery Hill was not assailable from the town, and I determined, with Johnson's division, to take possession of a wooded hill to my left, on a line with and commanding Cemetery Hill. Before Johnson got up, the enemy was reported moving to outflank our extreme left, and I could see that seemed to be his skirmishers in that direction.

I have the honor to remain, &c.,

R. S. EWELL,
Lieutenant-General,
Provisional Army, C. S. Army

---

rounded up, had fled to the rear. The result was that on the evening of the first day, the two Federal corps that had done the fighting could muster no more than 5,000 fighting men.

Although the first day of the Battle of Gettysburg was a Confederate victory, it too had been a costly one. Heth's 7,500-man division had suffered nearly 1,500 casualties. Where the fighting was thickest, individual units had suffered disproportionately. The 26th North Carolina suffered 75 percent casualties with only 212 of its 800 men surviving unscathed. Its F Company had suffered 100 percent casualties among its 90 officers and men.

The day had also ended with a serious difference of opinion between Lee and Longstreet. Longstreet was largely a defensive-minded general, and he had long-held concerns about Lee's invasion of the North. The invasion would work, Longstreet argued, only if once the Army of Northern Virginia crossed into Northern territory, Lee took up a strong defensive position that the Federals would be compelled to attack. With such an advantage the Confederates might gain another inexpensive victory like at Fredericksburg. Summing up his views, Longstreet wrote, "The plan of defensive tactics gave some hope of success, and, in fact, I assured General Lee that the First Corps would receive and defend the battle if he would guard our flanks, leaving the other corps to gather the fruits of success. The First Corps was as solid as a rock—a great rock. It was not to be broken of good position by direct assault, and was steady enough to work and wait for its chosen battle." For Longstreet, the overriding vision, both of the campaign and his corps, was clearly defensive.

Lee's Plan of Attack

As Lee had been waiting for Ewell to attack, Longstreet had ridden up. Lee told Longstreet he had ordered Ewell to seize Cemetery Hill and added that if Meade was still on the field the next day, Lee was going to attack. This strategy shocked Longstreet, who reiterated his thoughts on how the campaign should be fought. He recommended the Confederates move south and east across Meade's line of communications, find a strong defensive position, and force Meade into a costly attack.

Longstreet was surprised when Lee remained insistent upon attacking. He later wrote that he told Lee, "If we could have chosen a point to meet our plans of operation, I do not think we could have found a better one than that upon which they are now concentrating. All we have to do is to throw our army around by their left, and we shall interpose between the Federal army

RIGHT: This the first in a series of maps drawn by the U.S. Army's Chief of Engineers and published in 1876, showing the battlefield on July 1st, 2nd, and 3rd. The disposition of troops at the end of the first day's fighting gave the Federals the defender's advantage of central position and interior lines.

and Washington. We can get a strong position and wait, and if they fail to attack us we shall have everything in condition to move back tomorrow night in the direction of Washington, selecting beforehand a good position into which we can place our troops to receive battle next day. Finding our object is Washington or that army, the Federals will be sure to attack us. When they attack, we shall beat them, as we proposed to do before we left Fredericksburg, and the probabilities are that the fruits of our success will be great."

As Longstreet remembered it, upon starting the campaign Lee shared these views, but obviously Longstreet had misread Lee's intentions. Now, pointing toward Cemetery Hill, Lee said, "The enemy is there, and I am going to attack him there." Longstreet countered, "If he is there, it is because he is anxious that we should attack him—a good reason, in my judgment, for not doing so." Lee was unmoved. "I am going to whip them or they are going to whip me," he replied.

FACING PAGE: Taken shortly after the battle, this is the farmhouse used as the headquarters of General Robert E. Lee on the Chambersburg Pike.

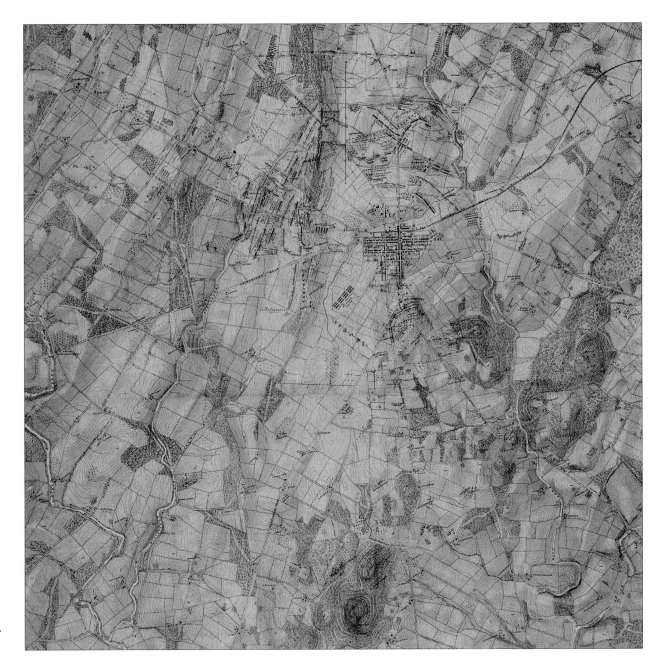

Day Two: Status Quo Maintained

The second day of the Battle of Gettysburg demonstrated the strength of the defense and the advantage of central position. The outcome of the day's fighting would best be declared a draw with Meade still holding key terrain and Lee still with plenty of fight left in him.

A fter just a few hours' sleep, Lee was up at 3:30 a.m. on July 2, eager to resume the attack as soon as possible. He dispatched two staff officers to observe the Round Tops and soon conducted his own survey from Seminary Ridge, noting that the Federal concentration around Cemetery Hill did not seem to extend much further south along Cemetery Ridge.

FACING PAGE: The 1st Minnesota are most remembered for their actions on July 2, where the regiment prevented the Confederates from capturing Cemetery Ridge.

RIGHT: Samuel Crawford and his Pennsylvania Reserve Division figured prominently in the fighting on July 2.

Cemetery Ridge stretched south of Gettysburg for some 2 miles (3.2 km). This was a low ridge, at some points dipping nearly to ground level. At the north end of this feature was Cemetery Hill, rising about 80 feet (25 m) above Gettysburg. Baltimore Pike flowed into Cemetery Hill from the southeast. To the east of Cemetery Hill was Culp's Hill, about 100 feet (30 m) higher. At the south end of Culp's Hill was Spangler's Spring, a natural water source. The road to Taneytown ran parallel to the ridge on the east side. At the south end was Little Round Top and below it, Big Round Top, which was sometimes referred to locally as Sugar Loaf.

Along the base of the two Round Tops, a small stream called Plum Run wound through

broken ground. The Round Tops formed the eastern face of Plum Run Valley, and Houck's Run, the largest spur coming off Cemetery Ridge, formed most of the western face. At the southern end of Houck's Ridge was a 10-acre (4 ha) jumble of huge granite boulders and slabs. An eerie cave or den deep in its bowels gave this area the name Devil's Den.

Federal Dispositions

The Federal line assumed the shape of a fishhook with the tip being at Culp's Hill, the hook curving around Cemetery Ridge, and the eye at the two Round Tops. Although Big Round Top was the taller of the two hills, Little Round Top had been recently cleared of timber, and therefore provided better observation and fields of fire. It would prove to be the key to the second day's fighting. Lee's men wrapped around the outside of the Federal fishhook, with Ewell in the north, Hill in the center, and Longstreet in the south. Such a configuration gave Meade key advantages in terms of observation and fields of fire as well as central position. Moreover, the checkerboard of fence-enclosed fields, woods, and orchards that lay in between the Round Tops and the Emmitsburg Road increased the difficulty of moving and controlling an attacking force.

As Lee studied this terrain, Longstreet joined him and renewed his arguments for a wide turning movement, but Lee remained committed to an attack. Indeed, there was a certain tension building as other commanders arrived to report their dispositions and receive instructions.

Longstreet's Corps was complete except for Major General George Pickett's division, which had been left behind to guard supplies at Chambersburg and would not reach Gettysburg until the afternoon. When Major General John Bell Hood arrived with his division, Longstreet told him that Lee "is a little nervous this morning. He wishes me to attack. I do not wish to do so without Pickett. I never like to go into battle with one boot off." There was more strain when Major General Lafayette McLaws arrived and received conflicting instructions from Lee and Longstreet about where to position his division. Longstreet was clearly still smarting from his inability to convince Lee to adopt his plan. Lee was also not in a good mood, perhaps due to a bout of diarrhea. The end result was that nerves were raw as the Confederate high command prepared for its next move.

Lee Orders the Attack

Lee soon received confirmation from the reconnaissance he had sent to the south that the Federal line did not extend far in that direction. Only pickets occupied the southern portion of Cemetery Ridge, and the Round Tops were thus far unmanned. Lee initially wanted Ewell to attack Cemetery and Culp's Hills on the Federal right, but Ewell expressed reservations. Instead, Lee ordered Longstreet to make the main attack against the left of the Federal line in the vicinity of the Little and Big Round Tops. Longstreet would then turn north and roll up the enemy flank. Ewell and Hill would make secondary attacks in

ABOVE: Lieutenant General Longstreet's Corps was at the center of the action on July 2. Longstreet himself showed little enthusiasm for Lee's offensive plans.

FACING PAGE: The 110-foot (33 m) high Pennsylvania Memorial, the largest on the battlefield, sits on Cemetery Ridge.

the north to prevent Meade from moving forces to confront Longstreet in the south.

Longstreet repeated his arguments against an attack, but Lee was not persuaded. At about 10:00 a.m. Lee told Longstreet "I think you better move on" and then rode off. In spite of his objections, Longstreet prepared to carry out his orders, but he certainly did so with no great sense of urgency. His hesitancy would later become a matter of controversy.

After the war, supporters of Lee and Longstreet would argue about whether or not Lee had ordered the second day's attack to begin at daylight. Major General Jubal Early, one of the early architects of the "Lost Cause" argument, first made the charge in a speech at Washington, D.C., and Lee University delivered January 19, 1872. He asserted that there was a conference held with Lee on July 1 involving Early, Ewell, and Rodes at which Lee "expressed his determination to assault the enemy's position at daylight on the next morning." Early reports Lee then left the group "for the purpose of ordering up Longstreet's Corps in time to begin the attack at dawn next morning."

After criticizing Longstreet for not attacking, Early contended "had the attack been made at daylight, as contemplated, it must have resulted in a brilliant victory." Early used his position as president of the Southern Historical Society to continue to publicize his thesis. Brigadier General William Pendleton, Lee's chief of artillery, joined Early in advancing the "sunrise attack" claim and generally disparaging Longstreet's performance at Gettysburg.

BELOW: While General Robert E. Lee surveys the Union position from Seminary Ridge, Lt. Colonel Charles Marshall, Major John W. Fairfax, and Lt. General A. P. Hill wait in the background. Lee would continue to experience difficulty getting his subordinate commanders to implement his plans on the second day at Gettysburg.

FACING PAGE: Federal cannon on Rocky Hill bombard Confederate formations on July 2. T. C. Porter honored the defenders of "The Rocky Hills of Gettysburg" in an 1864 song that proclaimed: "And age to age shall pass it down, The story of their bright renown, And everlasting fame shall crown, The rocky hills of Gettysburg."

BATTLE OF GETTYSBURG, THURSDAY EVENING, JULY 2, 1863, AS SEEN FROM ROCKY HILL, ON MEADE'S LEFT.—From a Sketch by Edwin Forbes.

There was never a more critical sunset in America than that of the 2d of July, 1863. The whole world knew that on the morrow the political fate of the American Republic would be put into the balance of destiny. The fighting on that day had been favorable to the Confederates. They had won nearly all along the line. The Federals were concentrating and confirming themselves on the line of the Round Tops, Cemetery Ridge, and Culp's Hill. The illustration on this page is from a sketch drawn on the evening before the great battle. The sketch was made from Rocky Hill, on the left of Meade's position, and looks over to the southwest, where the long lines of Longstreet, Hill and Johnston were ready and inclined forward, so to speak, full of spirit for the contest of the morrow.

LONGSTREET'S LETTER TO COLONEL WALTER TAYLOR CONCERNING THE "SUNRISE ATTACK"

New Orleans, LA
April 20, 1875

My Dear Colonel:

Upon reading an address by Mr. Pendleton, published in the December number of *Southern Magazine*, I saw for the first time that Gen. Lee had ordered me to attack the left of the Federal army at "sunrise," on the second day of the battle of Gettysburg.

It occurs to me that if Gen. Lee had any such idea as an attack at sunrise, you must surely be advised of it. Right sure am I that such an order was never delivered to me, and it is not possible for me to believe that he ever entertained an idea that I was to attack at that hour. My two divisions, nor myself did not reach Gen. Lee until 8 a.m. on the 2nd, and if he had intended to attack at sunrise he surely would have expressed some surprise, or made some allusion to his orders. Please do me the favor to let me know what you know of this sunrise attack . . .
.

I remain very respectfully yours,
James Longstreet

Longstreet fought back, soliciting testimonies from fellow Confederate officers and recording his side of the argument in his autobiography, *From Manassas To Appomattox: Memoirs Of The Civil War In America*. While Lee no doubt hoped Longstreet would have attacked earlier than he did, there is little extant evidence to support definitively a claim that Lee ordered a sunrise attack.

This postwar controversy notwithstanding, the fact remains that the attack did not occur in the morning, and Lee became increasingly impatient throughout the day. At about 10:00 a.m., he rode to Ewell's position. According to Lee's plan, Ewell was to begin his supporting attack upon hearing the sound of Longstreet's guns. Longstreet remained silent, and Ewell remained motionless. An exasperated Lee returned to his headquarters. Along the way he encountered Hill's artillery commander, Colonel R. Lindsay Walker, who recalled, "General Lee manifested more impatience than I ever saw him exhibit on any other occasion; he seemed very much disappointed and worried that the attack had not opened earlier."

Stuart's Foray

Certainly part of Lee's frustration was with Jeb Stuart. Lee had instructed the cavalryman on June 22, "If you find that [then commander of

FACING PAGE: At Gettysburg Jeb Stuart ill-advisedly tried to replicate the ride he made around McClellan's entire army during the Peninsula Campaign in 1862.

TAYLOR'S REPLY

Norfolk, VA April 28, 1875

Dear General:

I have received your letter of the 20th instant. I have not read the article of which you speak, nor have I ever seen any copy of General Pendleton's address; indeed, I have read little or nothing of what has been written since the war. In the first place, because I could not spare the time; and in the second, of those of whose writings I have heard I deem but very few entitled to any attention whatever. I can only say that I never before heard of "the sunrise attack" you were to have made as charged by General Pendleton. If such an order was given you I never knew of it, or it has strangely escaped my memory. I think it more than probable that if General Lee had had your troops available the evening previous to the day of which you speak, he would have ordered an early attack, but this does not touch the point at issue. I regard it as a great mistake on the part of those who, perhaps, because of political differences, now undertake to criticize and attack your war record. Such conduct is most ungenerous, and I am sure meets the disapprobation of all good Confederates with whom I have had the pleasure of associating in the daily walks of life.

Yours very respectfully,
W. H. Taylor

the Army of the Potomac Major General Joseph Hooker] is moving northward, and that two brigades can guard the Blue Ridge and take care of your rear, you can move with the other three into Maryland and take position on General Ewell's right, place yourself in communication with him, guard his flank, and keep him informed of the enemy's movements." The next day, Lee clarified Stuart's options. The future course depended on whether or not "General Hooker's army remains inactive." If Hooker continued his passivity, Stuart "would be able to judge whether you can pass around their army without hindrance, doing all the damage you can, and cross the river east of the mountains. In either case, after crossing the river, you must move on and feel the right of Ewell's Corps."

Stuart paid little attention to these cautions and instead appeared to see the opportunity to reenact his flamboyant ride around Major General George McClellan's army during the Peninsula Campaign and restore his reputation after the embarrassment at Brandy Station. On June 25 he left Salem (now Marshall), Virginia with three of his brigades. For the next eight days he was completely out of touch with Lee.

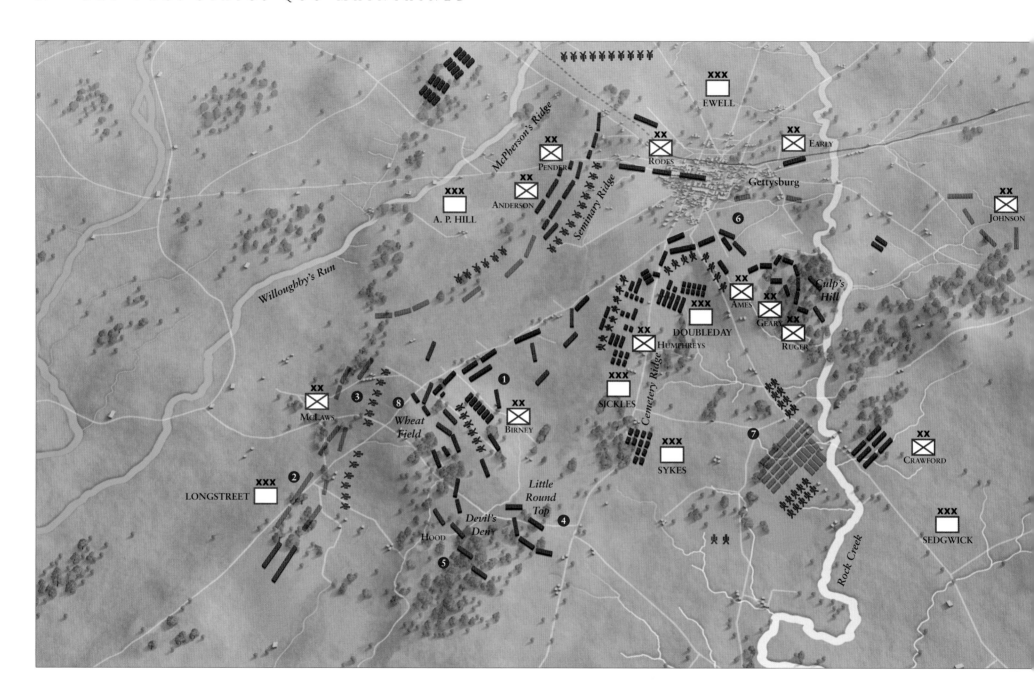

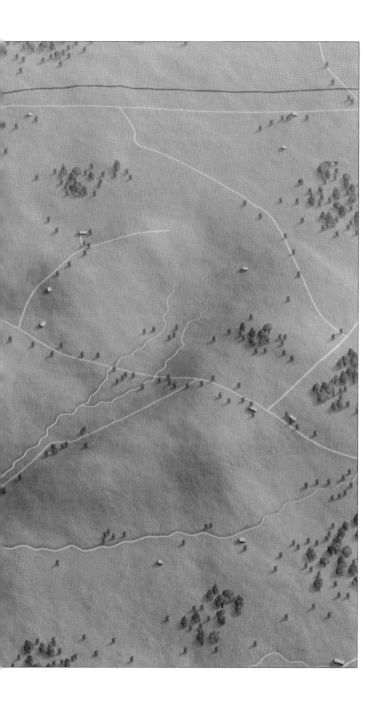

PHASE TWO
July 2

❶ On the second day of the battle, Sickles had ill-advisedly pushed his line forward, creating a vulnerable salient at the Peach Orchard.

❷ After failing to convince Lee to assume a defensive posture, a reluctant Longstreet finally attacked at about 4:30 p.m.

❸ At about 5:30 p.m., McLaws's division attacked into the salient in the Federal line.

❹ At around 3:00 p.m., Warren realized the key position at Little Round Top was unoccupied. He rushed Vincent's brigade there just in the nick of time.

❺ Oates's Alabamians of Hood's division were unable to dislodge Chamberlain's Federals from Little Round Top in an attack that if successful would have allowed the Confederates to roll up the Federal flank.

❻ Attacking some two hours after Longstreet, Ewell did little to divert Federal attention away from the main Confederate attack.

❼ The central position allowed Meade to move reinforcements to respond to Confederate attacks throughout the battlefield.

❽ The Wheat Field changed hands as many as seven times in the course of the fighting.

Limited Intelligence

The crisis of Stuart's absence to Lee was that cavalry was the principal intelligence-gathering organization during the Civil War. The advantage of the cavalry in this area was not just in its speed and mobility to gather information, but also its ability to rapidly return to friendly lines to report its findings. In these matters, the Confederacy enjoyed a tremendous initial advantage with Stuart providing the valuable and timely reconnaissance that Lee needed for his operational formulations. Now robbed of this asset, Lee suffered from a lack of the intelligence upon which he had come to rely. As Douglas Southall Freeman assessed the situation, Lee "had become dependent upon [Stuart] for information on the enemy's position and plans, and in Stuart's absence, he had no satisfactory form of military intelligence… The injudicious employment of the Confederate horse during the Gettysburg campaign was responsible for most of the other mistakes on the Southern side."

When Stuart finally returned to the army around noon on July 2, Lee was initially furious. "I have not heard a word from you for days," he scolded Stuart, "and you the eyes and ears of my army." When Stuart replied, "I have brought you 125 wagons and their teams, General," Lee admonished, "Yes, and they are an impediment to me now." Then Lee softened, telling Stuart, "We will not discuss this matter further. Help me fight these people." By then, however, it was too late for Stuart's strung-out column to join the fight that day.

RIGHT: Although Sickles performed poorly at Gettysburg, he was instrumental in preserving the battlefield after the war.

To Lee's further chagrin, Longstreet was waiting for the arrival of Brigadier General Evander Law's brigade and had not even moved his corps into its attack position. It was noon before Longstreet began to move and once started, his effort quickly encountered difficulty. Upon reaching Herr's Ridge, Brigadier General Joseph Kershaw, who was leading the march, realized that he would come under observation from the enemy if he continued forward. He ordered a halt, and Longstreet soon came up to assess the situation. Frustrated, Longstreet had little choice but to order a countermarch back toward Chambersburg Pike and then to an alternate route along Willoughby Run. This development caused another two-hour delay and it was not until 3:30 p.m. that Longstreet's Corps began moving into its attack position west of the Emmitsburg Road with Hood's division on the right and McLaws's on the left.

The Federals Prepare

The Confederate attack did not begin until 4:30 p.m., and by then the Federals had the opportunity to recover from a serious error in which Dan Sickles had failed to cover the key Little Round Top with his III Corps. The vulnerability was not discovered until 3:00 p.m. when Meade and Warren reconnoitered the III Corps lines.

Howard's XI Corps, Slocum's XII Corps, and what was left of I Corps held a line from Culp's Hill through Cemetery Hill. Hancock's II Corps occupied Ziegler's Grove and the open ridge immediately south of it. Meade wanted Sickles to put his III Corps in beside Hancock to hold whatever part of the ridge Hancock could not cover and also to occupy the Round Tops. Sykes's V Corps was in a position behind Cemetery Hill as the army's reserve. It was a good plan, but Sickles was not happy with his portion of it.

Sickles had been ordered to relieve Brigadier General John Geary's division of the XII Corps on Cemetery Ridge at about 5:00 a.m. Geary had occupied that position the previous evening and had placed two of his regiments on Little Round Top where he astutely believed the Confederates would have "an opportunity of enfilading our entire left wing and center with a fire which could not fail to dislodge us." Before leaving to join the rest of the XII Corps at Culp's Hill, Geary sent an aide to impress upon Sickles the importance of this position. Sickles dismissed the advice, noting that he would "attend to it in due time." Geary sent another message which Sickles also ignored. By then Geary had no other choice but to depart for Culp's Hill and leave Little Round Top undefended.

Sickles was a political general with a background as a lawyer rather than a professional soldier. He had won national attention in 1859 when he was acquitted of murdering his wife's lover by using the novel defense of temporary insanity. Whatever Sickles's legal skill, Meade had little respect for him as a general, and at 6:00 a.m. Meade sent his aide and son, Captain George Meade, to check on Sickles. When the young Meade returned to

report that Sickles was not sure where to deploy his troops, he was dispatched again to inform Sickles he was to occupy the line Geary had vacated. This time Captain Meade found Sickles inspecting the ground with dissatisfaction and fearful that Confederate guns could wreak havoc on it from the higher elevations offered at the Peach Orchard a half mile (0.8 km) to the west.

BELOW: Confederate troops advance toward Little Round Top. If the Confederates captured Little Round Top, the Federal flank was in danger of being rolled up.

EXCERPT FROM BERDAN'S OFFICIAL REPORT OF HIS SHARPSHOOTERS' ACTIONS ON JULY 2

HEADQUARTERS FIRST U.S. SHARPSHOOTERS,
July 29, 1863

Capt. F. BIRNEY,
Assistant Adjutant-General.

CAPTAIN: I have the honor to submit the following report of the operations of the Sharpshooters at the battle near Gettysburg:

On the morning of July 2, I received instructions from the division commander to assume command of the First and Second Regiments of Sharpshooters, and to report direct to division headquarters. In accordance with instructions received, I posted the Second Regiment, Major Stoughton commanding, on our left, to act as flankers, and the First Regiment on our front.

About 7.30 a.m. I received orders to send forward a detachment of 100 sharpshooters to discover, if possible, what the enemy was doing. I went out with the detail, and posted them on the crest of the hill beyond the Emmitsburg Road, and where they kept up a constant fire nearly all day upon the enemy in the woods beyond until they were driven in, about 5 p.m., by a heavy force of the enemy, after having expended all their ammunition.

As it was impossible with this force to proceed far enough to discover what was being done by

the enemy in the rear of this woods, I reported the fact to Major-General Birney, and about 11 a.m. I received an order from him to send out another detachment of 100 sharpshooters farther to the left of our lines, and to take the Third Maine

Volunteers as support, with directions to feel the enemy, and to discover their movements, if possible.

I moved down the Emmitsburg Road some distance beyond our extreme left and deployed the sharpshooters in a line running nearly east and west, and moved forward in a northerly direction parallel with the Emmitsburg Road. We soon came upon the enemy, and drove them sufficiently to discover three columns in motion in rear of the woods, changing direction, as it were, by the right flank. We attacked them vigorously on the flank, and from our having come upon them very unexpectedly, and getting close upon them, we were enabled to do great execution, and threw them for a time into confusion. They soon rallied, however, and attacked us, when, having accomplished the object of the reconnaissance, I withdrew under cover of the woods, bringing off most of our wounded, and reported about 2 o'clock to Major-General Birney the result of our operations and discoveries.

I have the honor to be, captain, your obedient servant,

H. BERDAN,
Colonel,
Commanding U.S. Sharpshooters

LEFT: The rocks of Devil's Den formed a natural defensive barrier for the Union troops.

brigade of Hill's Corps in Pitzer's Woods on the southern end of Seminary Ridge near where it terminates at the Millerstown Road. The sharpshooters reported an overestimated Confederate presence to Sickles, who incorrectly assumed he was facing a much larger force. In response, at 3:00 p.m. he pushed forward his corps to the Emmitsburg Road to meet what he thought was a major Confederate advance. In reality, Longstreet's Corps was still miles away.

Exposed Flank

Sickles's move, conducted without Meade's order or knowledge, isolated the II Corps about a half of a mile (0.8 km) in front of the rest of the army and created a salient that exposed Hancock's left flank. In the midst of this move, Meade called his corps commanders to a council of war, which Sickles declined to attend because of his present activity. Meade reiterated his order and about the time Sickles finally arrived at the meeting, fire could be heard from the south. Before Sickles could even dismount, Meade ordered him back to his troops to meet the attack. Meade also directed Sykes to hurry the V Corps forward to support Sickles.

Meade and his chief engineer Gouverneur Warren then rode to inspect the Federal left. They arrived under Confederate artillery fire to find Sickles in the Peach Orchard. Quickly assessing the danger, Meade told Sickles,

Sickles requested General Meade come to inspect the situation, and when Meade failed to come, Sickles rode to him. After a brief exchange, Meade sent his chief of artillery, Brigadier General Henry Hunt, to go back with Sickles.

Hunt agreed with Sickles that possession of the Peach Orchard and Devil's Den would be advantageous to the enemy, but when Sickles asked if he should move forward, Hunt claimed to lack the authority to give such an order. He did suggest Sickles send out skirmishers, and Sickles quickly dispatched four companies of the 1st U.S. Sharpshooters to check for advancing Confederates. Upon crossing the Emmitsburg Road, the Federals encountered three regiments belonging to Brigadier General Cadmus Wilcox's

FACING PAGE: Meade made his headquarters in the Leister farmhouse during the Battle of Gettysburg.

"General, I am afraid you are too far out." When Sickles tried to explain his search for higher ground, Meade tersely replied, "General Sickles, this is in some respects higher ground than that to the rear, but there is still higher in front of you, and if you keep on advancing you will find constantly higher ground all the way to the mountains."

Warren had an excellent understanding of the military value of terrain. He was also able to take a larger view of the Federal situation while Meade focused on the problem caused by Sickles. As they rode up, Warren pointed to Cemetery Ridge and noted, "Here is where our line should be," but Meade only replied, "It is too late now." Still, Meade's trust in Warren was complete and he told him, "I wish you would ride over and if anything serious is going on, attend to it."

With that, Warren rode off in the direction of Little Round Top. From that vantage point Warren could see the Confederates forming to attack the undefended Federal position. "The discovery," he wrote later, "was intensely thrilling to my feelings, and almost appalling." Realizing the criticality of the situation, Warren rushed into action and hurried Brigadier General Strong Vincent and his brigade to the scene. Colonel Joshua Chamberlain's 20th Maine, the advanced regiment of Vincent's brigade, arrived about 10 minutes before

Colonel William Oates and his 15th Alabama Regiment attacked his position.

The Confederates Attack

Oates's regiment was part of Hood's division. Advancing from Pitzer's Woods, Hood could see the Federals in the Peach Orchard, and his scouts told him the enemy line stretched all the way to Devil's Den. If he attacked north along

BELOW: Meade's capable engineer, Gouverneur Warren, recognized the criticality of Little Round Top.

ABOVE: When Longstreet finally attacked, the Confederates and Federals clashed in the Peach Orchard.

the Emmitsburg Road according to Lee's plan, Hood knew he would be trapped in enfilading fire from the right. Three times he asked Longstreet to instead skirt around the southern edge of the Round Tops and attack Cemetery Ridge from the flank and rear. Each time Longstreet unimaginatively told him Lee's orders must be obeyed. Unwilling to expose his division to such danger, Hood disobeyed and attacked eastward toward the Devil's Den and the Round Tops in a frontal rather than an oblique attack.

Hood advanced in two lines. On the right was Brigadier General Evander Law's Alabama brigade with Brigadier General Henry Benning's Georgia brigade behind him. On the left was Brigadier General Jerome Robertson's Texas brigade backed by Brigadier General George Anderson's Georgia brigade. The changed Confederate plan resulted in a piecemealed attack, and the rough terrain further compartmentalized the effort into a highly individualized struggle.

Facing Robertson, the division of Major General David Birney occupied the left half of Sickles's salient. Birney had three brigades arranged in an irregularly-shaped and overextended line from the Peach Orchard southeast down a little slope and across the Wheat Field up to Devil's Den. Brigadier

General Charles Graham's brigade was on the right, Colonel Regis de Trobriand's was in the center, and Brigadier General John Hobart Ward's was on the left. Birney's line was especially thin, and he had no reserves.

With a force close to 2,200 men organized in six regiments with two companies of sharpshooters, Ward's brigade was the largest in the III Corps. Ward was a veteran commander with a solid reputation. His sector covered the boulder-strewn Devil's Den. On the extreme left of the entire Army of the Potomac was Captain James Smith's New York Independent Battery overlooking Devil's Den. Ward had the 4th Maine and 124th New York supporting Smith's battery on his left, and the rest of his brigade to the north along Houck's Ridge.

Robertson's men advanced through Rose's Woods with the 3rd Arkansas and 1st Texas in the lead. Benefiting from the natural cover, the Federals put up a stubborn defense. "As fast as we would break one line of the enemy," Robertson remembered, "another fresh one would present itself."

Robertson's attack got some help when the 44th and 48th Alabama Regiments from Law's brigade threatened Ward's left flank with an attack up the Plum Run Valley. Under heavy attack, Smith implored his gunners to "Give them shell! Give them solid shot! Damn them, give them anything!" The 124th New York came to Smith's aid with a counterattack, but by then Benning's brigade had come up to join the attack. Anderson's brigade hurried forward and came alongside Benning's left and smashed into de Trobriand's brigade.

Excerpt from the Diary of Private John Wilkerson, Company H, 3rd Arkansas Regiment, Recording the Action at Devil's Den

By evening our ranks were getting thin. It was fight all the time. Each side wanted the protection of those rocks. One in particular, it was very large, about four or five feet high. I saw smoke coming from behind that one and made a run for it, swerving to the right, with my gun ready. I cried, "Hands up," they dropped their guns and came out from behind the rock. There were six of them. One said,

LEFT: His decisive leadership at Little Round Top made Colonel Strong Vincent one of the Federal heroes on July 2. As Brigadier General Law's brigade charged towards them, Vincent encouraged his men by calling to them, "Don't give an inch boys."

"Young man, where is your troops?" I told them I was it, and showed them to the rear, and saw to it that they went. I went for that same rock, but went on the wrong side, right into the muzzle of the Yank's gun. He could easily put his gun in my face. He jabbed the gun out and fired, but it didn't touch me. Then he threw the gun up and begged me to spare his life. At that instant a comrade came on the other side of the rock and would have shot the Yank, had I not stopped him.

Birney desperately tried to find rein-forcements wherever he could to counter the Confederate threat. The combat was intense, and the rocky ground on the verge of Plum Run would become known as the "Slaughter Pen." Colonel Thomas Egan's 40th New York suffered more than a third casualties and was forced to fall back. The 6th New Jersey, the other unit Birney had rushed to the scene, covered the retreat and then withdrew as well. In what one Texan described as "one of the wildest, fiercest struggles of the war," Hood's division had secured the Devil's Den area and a lodgement on Houck's Ridge.

On the far right of Law's line, Oates's 15th Alabama was under fire from Federal sharpshooters toward the base of Big Round Top. Oates's men charged and overcame this

LEFT: A contemporary photograph showing the body of a Confederate soldier in Devil's Den, probably taken shortly after the battle.

resistance about halfway up the slope. It was hard work with the Federals firing from behind rocks and trees, then withdrawing to similar positions and firing some more. By the time Oates's men reached the 305-foot (93 m) summit, they were exhausted.

Oates paused for a few minutes to let his men catch their breath while he looked over the terrain. He saw a few Federal signalmen on Little Round Top and quickly realized the significance of this piece of terrain. While he was contemplating his next move, a courier arrived with the news that Hood had been wounded and Law was now in command. The general's orders were for Oates to attack Little Round Top.

Little Round Top

Between Big and Little Round Top was a 500 yard (460 m) saddle, and as Oates descended into it he did not see a single enemy soldier on Little Round Top. Along the way, he was joined by three more Confederate regiments that had maneuvered around Devil's Den and the western base of Big Round Top. Now, as Oates began to climb up the southeastern slope of Little Round Top, he was met by "the most destructive fire I ever saw" from Chamberlain's newly arrived and well-covered Maine regiment less than 50 yards (45 m) to Oates's front.

Oates tried to get out of this devastating fire by working his way around the Federal left flank, but Chamberlain countered by dropping his left wing back to form a V-shaped position. The fighting became desperate, and Chamberlain

ordered his men to charge, personally leading them with his sword drawn. At nearly the same time, the Alabamians began receiving fire from their rear from the sharpshooters they had fought through earlier. Oates had little choice but to abandon his attack.

The 20th Maine suffered 130 casualties in the fight, over one third of its 386-man strength. Such a great sacrifice was critical to the Federal cause. Had the Confederates been able to gain Little Round Top, they could have rolled up

ABOVE: The men of the 5th Texas Regiment storm Little Round Top. The Confederates attacked Little Round Top, hoping to roll up the Federal flank.

the Federal flank along Cemetery Ridge. Chamberlain saved the day for the Federals and won the Medal of Honor for his heroic actions.

While Hood's division was battling on the right, Longstreet's other division, the one commanded by McLaws, was fighting on the left. This was a weak part of Sickles's line where he had a division commanded by Brigadier General Andrew Humphreys deployed along the Emmitsburg Road, and the right side of Birney's division, which had Graham and de Trobriand's brigades on either side of the Millerstown Road. Unfortunately for Lee, however, his plan had lost its synchronization, and by the time Longstreet unleashed McLaws at about 5:30 p.m., Hood's attack had passed its prime. The Confederate attack on July 2 simply failed to press the Federals in a way that prevented Meade from using his interior lines to full effect.

The Peach Orchard and Wheat Field

The brigade on McLaws's right was commanded by Joseph Kershaw. Longstreet moved with Kershaw as far as the Emmitsburg Road and then waved the South Carolinians forward. Crossing the road, three of Kershaw's regiments wheeled north to attack the Federal line in the

FACING PAGE: Colonel Joshua Chamberlain won the Medal of Honor for his leadership of the 20th Maine at Little Round Top.

RIGHT: A former college professor Chamberlain served as Governor of Maine after the Civil War.

Peach Orchard while two others joined Anderson in attacking de Trobriand's small brigade in the Wheat Field. Brigadier General Paul Semmes's brigade followed about 10 minutes behind Kershaw. De Trobriand's position became untenable when Brigadier General James Barnes, without informing de Trobriand, ordered his V Corps division to withdraw from de Trobriand's right. With his flank exposed, de Trobriand was forced to fall back. The exuberant Confederates rushed across the Wheat Field in de Trobriand's wake only to meet fresh Federal reinforcements commanded by Brigadier General John Caldwell. These men had been rushed to the scene by Hancock from the II Corps' sector.

The urgency of the situation precluded Caldwell from doing anything more sophisticated than hurling his brigades into the fight one after another. First came Colonel Edward Cross's brigade. Cross was mortally wounded in the attack. Then came Brigadier General Samuel Zook who had to work his way through Barnes's retreating V Corps division. Yelling "If you can't get out of the way, lie down and we will march over you," Zook charged into the Wheat Field. He was also mortally wounded. Next the Irish Brigade of Colonel Patrick Kelly plunged into the gap between Cross's and Zook's men. Before the attack, the brigade's chaplain, Father William Corby,

LEFT: In delaying the Confederate onslaught, Andrew Humphreys claimed that "twenty times did I bring my men to a halt and face about."

had admonished the men that "the Catholic Church refuses Christian burial to the soldier who turns his back upon the foe." Finally, Caldwell committed his last brigade, one commanded by Colonel John Brooke, just 24 years old. Brooke's charge succeeded in halting Semmes's Georgians temporarily.

As Semmes's men rallied, another Georgia brigade commanded by Brigadier General William Wofford crashed into Caldwell's right flank. It was a seesaw battle back and forth, but eventually the tide turned in the favor of the Federals. As Brooke reported, "Pressing forward, firing as we went, we drove back the first line of the enemy, capturing a great number, and then charging the second line, drove it from its almost impregnable position on a rocky crest." By one count, the Wheat Field changed hands seven times over the course of the fighting, but it ended up in Federal control.

Exploiting the Gap

Brigadier General William Barksdale's Mississippi brigade had preceded Wofford's attack into the Wheat Field with its own attack directly into the Federal defenses at the Peach Orchard. There he found the gap between Graham's and de Trobriand's brigades.

Barksdale's left-most units broke the Federal line just north of the Peach Orchard and then wheeled left to attack the enemy along the Emmitsburg Road at the Sherfy buildings. Barksdale's right wing and Wofford's brigade hit the orchard head on. The 2nd New Hampshire Regiment was caught between the Confederate pincers and was forced to retreat. The Federal artillery was also forced back, and the Confederates were able to seize the high ground in the orchard.

Barksdale urged his men forward against Brigadier General Andrew Humphreys's division along the Emmitsburg Road. Alone and outnumbered, the Federals were forced to retreat, but Humphreys's commanding presence made the withdrawal an orderly one. He finally made it back to the crest of Cemetery Ridge where his men fell in on the left of the II Corps line. Humphreys had lost more than 2,000 of his 5,000 men in the running battle, but he had bought valuable time for the Federal command.

Attack on Cemetery Ridge

Having crushed the III Corps' right, the Confederate wave now swept toward Cemetery Ridge. With Barksdale and Wofford decisively engaged, Longstreet had committed all his available units. A. P. Hill's Corps now took up the attack with Brigadier General Richard Anderson's division. Leading the way was

FACING PAGE: The Wheat Field changed hands as many as seven times during the fighting. Colonel Harrison Jeffords was mortally wounded there protecting the 4th Michigan's flag.

FACING PAGE: Hobart Ward's brigade, under attack here by Joseph Kershaw's Confederates, lost more than a third of its men.

BELOW: Brigadier General Samuel Kosciuzko Zook was badly wounded on July 2 as he led his brigade on horseback into the Wheat Field. He died the next day.

Brigadier General Ambrose Wright and his 1,413-man brigade preparing to storm Cemetery Ridge.

Meade, however, had the advantage of central position. Arrayed along his 3-mile (5 km) long fish-hook shaped line, Meade had an average of 17,000 infantrymen per mile. On the outside of that arc, Lee had a line some 2 miles (3.2 km) longer that averaged only 10,000 men per mile. Meade

ABOVE: Captain John Bigelow's 9th Massachusetts artillery battery fought a valiant rear guard action against Barksdale's brigade near the Trostle Farm to buy precious time for the Federals.

used this geographical advantage, as well as the disjointed nature of the Confederate attacks, to rush reinforcements from quieter sectors to more threatened points on the battlefield.

This notion of central position was critical to the military theorist Antione Henri, Baron de

FACING PAGE: Urging his Mississippians forward with his hat in his hand, William Barksdale led his brigade into the 114th Pennsylvania near the Sherfy House.

Jomini's geometric approach to warfare. Jomini was so influential during the Civil War that one historian claimed, "Many a Civil War general went into battle with a sword in one hand and Jomini's *Summary of the Art of War* in the other." For Jomini, the problem was to bring the maximum possible force to bear against an inferior enemy force at the decisive point. He explained, "If your strategic positions are more closely connected than the enemy's, you can concentrate more rapidly and more easily than he can..." This condition could best be achieved by properly ordering one's lines of communication relative to the enemy's so that the friendly force possessed "interior lines." Interior lines allowed the friendly commander to move parts of his army more rapidly than an enemy could operating on exterior lines. In this way the force operating on interior lines could defeat in detail an enemy operating on exterior lines. Meade enjoyed this advantage at Gettysburg.

The Federal left and center were currently the most hard-pressed, and Meade used his advantage of interior lines to relieve the pressure. He sent two more V Corps brigades to help Vincent and Chamberlain consolidate their hold on Little Round Top. Most of XII Corps marched to the sound of the guns from Culp's Hill. Two divisions from I Corps moved forward

from their positions behind Cemetery Hill. The VI Corps provided three brigades from the army's reserve. Brigadier General Henry Hunt scrounged enough artillery to defend a line on a low rise just east of Plum Run. Thus as the Confederate line surged forward toward Cemetery Ridge, it was continually met by reinforcements that had arrived only moments before. Finally a counterattack by Brigadier General Samuel Crawford's Pennsylvania Reserve Division forced the Confederates back to the Wheat Field.

Barksdale's attack was also running out of steam. Colonel George Willard's brigade from Hancock's II Corps attacked just west of Plum Run and drove Barksdale back, but the Confederate artillery under Colonel Edward Porter Alexander that had moved forward to the high ground by the Emmitsburg Road evened the score. On the Federal side, Lieutenant Colonel Freeman McGilvery gathered enough of the artillery reserve to form a line of two dozen guns just behind Plum Run. It was a fierce battle that left both Willard and Barksdale dead, but in the end, the Confederate attack was stopped.

Charge of the 1st Minnesotas

One last threat came as Brigadier General Cadmus Wilcox's brigade found a gap left in the Federal line where troops had been sent to

ABOVE: Antoine Henri Jomini, Swiss military officer and military theorist, championed the importance of interior lines and central position.

FACING PAGE: Confederate infantry from A. P. Hill's Corps charge toward the ornate gate of Evergreen Cemetery on Cemetery Hill.

BELOW: The 1st Minnesota suffered the highest percentage of casualties of any Federal regiment during the war, but did their duty on July 2.

fight elsewhere. Hancock rushed Colonel William Colville's 1st Minnesota Regiment into action, pointing to the Confederate flag and ordering, "Advance, Colonel, and take those colors." The Minnesotans charged in a column of fours and knocked the Confederates off guard. Recovering from the initial shock, the Confederates used their superior numbers to work their way around both flanks of the Minnesotans' line. This maneuver—called a "double envelopment"—left the Federals trapped in a wall of fire. Only the well-placed canister of McGilvery's guns saved the Minnesotans from complete annihilation. This desperate effort succeeded in repulsing the Confederate attack, but the cost was terrible. Of the 262 men of the 1st Minnesota engaged, 82 percent became casualties; the highest losses of any Federal regiment in the war. Richard Moe's history of the regiment is aptly titled *The Last Full Measure*.

By darkness, Meade's forces had halted the Confederate attack on Cemetery Ridge. Someone observed that it had been a close call, to which a thankful Meade replied, "Yes, but it is all right now, it is all right now."

Stalemate

On the other end of the line, Ewell had finally heard the sound of Longstreet's guns and began the attack Lee had intended to divert Federal attention away from Longstreet's main effort. While he had been waiting, Ewell had done little to prepare his corps or inform his division commanders. After initiating an ineffective artillery barrage, Ewell launched uncoordinated attacks on Cemetery and Culp's Hills at about 6:30 p.m.

This was some two hours after Longstreet had started his attack, and by this time, most of the Federals on Culp's Hill and about half of those on Cemetery Hill had been redeployed to thwart Confederate attacks elsewhere—exactly

the development Lee had intended Ewell's attack to prevent. Apparently, Ewell intended an echeloned attack from left to right. Johnson would initiate by attacking toward Culp's Hill, followed by Early attacking Cemetery Hill, and then Rodes attacking Cemetery Hill from the northwest. Opposing Johnson's 5,000 men were 1,310 entrenched Federals under Brigadier General George Sears Greene. Sears was 62 years old, but he still had the heart of a fighter. Moreover, he had considerable experience as a civil engineer and was an expert of building field fortifications. Under his direction, his men had prepared 5-foot (1.5 m) high breastworks of earth and logs.

Breastwork Defences

As Greene's men would soon demonstrate, the combination of the rifle and the breastwork had given the defense a marked advantage over the offense during the Civil War. To build breastworks, companies would fell and trim

ABOVE: Winfield Scott Hancock was instrumental in rushing Federal units to threatened sectors.

FACING PAGE: After nightfall, the Louisiana Tiger Brigade overwhelmed Rickett's Pennsylvania Battery on East Cemetery Hill but could not solidify their victory when reinforcements did not arrive and a supporting attack to the west did not materialize.

EXCERPT FROM HANCOCK'S OFFICIAL REPORT OF THE FIGHTING ON JULY 2

Brig. Gen. S. WILLIAMS,
Assistant Adjutant-General, Army of the Potomac

GENERAL: I directed General Humphreys to form his command on the ground from which General Caldwell had moved to the support of the Third Corps, which was promptly done. The number of his troops collected was, however, very small, scarcely equal to an ordinary battalion, but with many colors, this small command being composed of the fragments of many shattered regiments. Three guns of one of its batteries had been left on the field, owing to the losses of horses and men. I established Colonel Willard's brigade at the point through which General Birney's division had retired, and fronting the approach of the enemy, who were pressing vigorously on. There were no other troops on its right or left, and the brigade soon became engaged, losing its commander, Colonel Willard, and many officers and men.

At this juncture, reinforcements, for which I had previously sent to General Meade by a staff officer, consisting of a part of General Newton's corps (Doubleday's division and the remnant of Robinson's), arrived, established themselves on the line, meeting the enemy at once, and doing good execution.

Proceeding along the line, I met a regiment of the enemy, the head of whose column was about passing through an unprotected interval in our line. A fringe of undergrowth in front of the line offered facilities for it to approach very close to our lines without being observed. It was advancing firing, and had already twice wounded my aide, Captain Miller. The First Minnesota Regiment coming up at this moment, charged the rebel regiment in handsome style, capturing its colors, and driving it back in disorder.

I cannot speak too highly of this regiment and its commander in its attack, as well as in its subsequent advance against the enemy, in which it lost three-fourths of the officers and men engaged. One of the regiments of the Vermont Brigade afterward advanced upon its right, and retook the guns of one of the reserve batteries, from which the cannoneers and supports had been driven.

I have the honor to be, very respectfully, your obedient servant,

WINF'D S. HANCOCK,
Major General,
Commanding Second Corps

trees and then roll the logs into a line to form a timber revetment usually 4 feet (1.2 m) high. This structure was then banked with earth from a ditch dug to its front. The result was a sloping parapet about 7 to 10 feet (2-3 m) thick at the top and an additional 3 feet (1 m) at the bottom. On top of the revetment was a line of headlogs positioned to leave a horizontal loophole about 3 inches (7.5 cm) wide through which to fire. The trees and bushes in front of the breastwork were then felled outward to create an obstacle that sometimes was augmented by a chevaux-de-frise or sharpened palisades. The drill became such a matter of routine that a company could cover itself within an hour of halting, even without engineer support.

With the benefit of this protection, Greene's men repulsed three attacks from the brigades of Brigadier General John Jones and Colonel J. M. Williams. Only Brigadier General George Steuart had any success, capturing some vacant trenches Sears was too understrength to man. Steuart, however, was unable to advance any further.

Excerpt from "The Breastworks at Culp's Hill" By Captain Jesse Jones of the 60th New York

The men restrained their nervous fingers; the hostile guns flamed out against us not fifteen yards in front. Our men from the front were tumbling over the breastwork, and for a breathless moment those behind the breastwork waited. Then out into the night like chain-lightning leaped the zigzag line of fire. Now was the value of breastworks apparent, for, protected by these, few of our men were hit, and feeling a sense of security, we worked with corresponding energy. Without breastworks our line would have been swept away in an instant by the hailstorm of bullets and the flood of men. The enemy worked still farther around to our right, entered the breastwork beyond our line, and crumpled up and drove back, a short distance, our extreme right regiment. They advanced a little way, but were checked by the fire of a couple of small regiments borrowed for the emergency from General Wadsworth, and placed in echelon.

BELOW: Confederates work their way up Culp's Hill where New Yorkers fighting behind the protection of breastworks await them.

FACING PAGE: Longstreet's attack as seen from the Federal positions. On the second day of Gettysburg, the Confederate attack lacked unity of effort and cohesion.

BELOW: Federal troops defend Cemetery Hill. When Rodes failed to attack on the west, Early's men had to forfeit their gains on East Cemetery Hill.

Attack Repulsed

Early's men attacked after Johnson, and they fared a little better. The Confederates routed a line of Federals and soon were ascending Cemetery Hill; the Federal guns were unable to lower their elevation sufficiently to stop and engage them. This success, however, was short lived when Major General Schurz sent reinforcements that drove the Confederates back down the slope. However, when Colonel Samuel Sprigg Carroll arrived with his 1st Brigade (3rd Division), the matter was settled. After only a few minutes fighting, the Confederates ceased their attack. Rodes, whose division had not even completely left Gettysburg until after dark, decided not to enter the fray. Neither Longstreet

THE BATTLE OF GETTYSBURG—LONGSTREET'S ATTACK UPON OUR LEFT CENTRE—BLUE RIDGE IN THE DISTANCE.—From a Drawing by Mr. A. R. Waud.—[See Page 510.]

ABOVE: This circa 1909 photograph taken from Cemetery Ridge shows a panorama of the second day's battle.

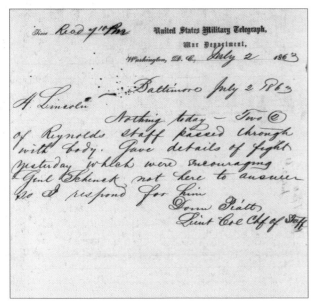

LEFT: The telegraph allowed government authorities to keep abreast of battlefield events such as via this report to President Lincoln of the second day's fighting.

nor Ewell had met any success, and the second day's fighting ended in a stalemate.

At 8:00 p.m., Meade had cabled Washington, "I shall remain in my present position tomorrow." After this initial decision, he had to add details to the plan, and at 11:00 p.m., he called a council of war. His subordinate commanders favored remaining in position but not launching an offensive. Meade agreed. The Federals would hold their ground and wait for Lee to attack. As the meeting adjourned, Meade warned Brigadier General John Gibbon, whose II Corps division occupied the center of the Federal line, "If Lee attacks tomorrow, it will be to your front." When Gibbon asked why, Meade replied, "Because he has made attacks on both our flanks and failed, and if he concludes to try it again, it will be on our center." The next day's events would make Meade appear prophetic.

If the second day of Gettysburg had brought relief and perhaps a small dose of confidence to Meade, it had been marked by frustration on many fronts for Lee. Simply put, Lee had been unable to influence his subordinates to behave as he wished. Stuart had left him without the intelligence upon which Lee had so come to depend. Ewell had not shown the initiative Lee had become used to with Jackson. Longstreet did not share Lee's offensive vision and had acted unenthusiastically.

Lee must also shoulder part of the blame for the day's poor outcome. He had developed a complicated plan that he lacked the staff to oversee. His verbal orders were unclear to his subordinates. His echelon sequence seemed to be unable to sustain itself if the attack of a given division stalled. Moreover, like several of his subordinate commanders, Lee had taken little active role in controlling the unfolding events. The result was an extremely disjointed attack that Meade was able to defeat by using his central position and the hard-fighting of his men.

RIGHT: At the end of the second day's fighting, Meade held strong defensive positions and was ready if Lee attacked again. Produced in 1876, this original map reads: "The map is reduced from one on a scale of 200 feet to the inch, deposited in the Archives of the office of the Chief of Engineers. The survey was ordered by Brevet Major General A. A. Humphreys, Chief of Engineers, and conducted under Brevet Major General G. K. Warren, Major of Engineers." Drainage, vegetation, roads, railroads, fences, houses with names of residents, and a detailed plan of the town of Gettysburg are shown. "Every object is represented here as near as possible as it was at the time of the battle." Dotted lines and arrows indicate troop movements.

Day Three: Federal Victory

The third and final day of the Battle of Gettysburg featured the famous Pickett's Charge in which Lee made one last effort to gain victory. Again the strength of the defense prevailed and the Federals carried the day and the battle. Lee was left with no choice but to withdraw back to Virginia.

I n spite of the disappointment that Lee must have felt over the second day's failure, he remained confident. Casualties had been heavy on both sides, but the second day had hit the Federals especially hard. In fact, 65 percent of Meade's total losses at Gettysburg occurred on July 2. Having struck the Federal right the first day and the left the second, Lee—as Meade had predicted—now resolved to attack

FACING PAGE: One of the iconic images of Pickett's Charge is Lewis Armistead leading his men to the "High Water Mark of the Confederacy."

RIGHT: George Custer was instrumental in foiling Stuart's attempt to outflank Meade's army on July 3.

the Federal center. Major General George Pickett's 6,000-man division had not been engaged in the first two days' fighting. Released from his mission of guarding the army's supply wagons at Chambersburg, Pickett marched his 15 Virginia regiments across South Mountain. About 6:00 p.m. on July 2, he halted at a point 4 miles (6.5 km) west of Gettysburg and asked Lee if he should rest his tired men or press forward to join the fight. "Tell General Pickett," Lee replied, "I shall not want him this evening; to let his men rest, and I will send him word when I want him."

Fighting on Culp's Hill

Lee developed a plan to have Longstreet, with Pickett's fresh division, attack the Federal center

at Cemetery Ridge while Ewell attacked southward from Culp's Hill on the Federal right flank. Stuart's newly arrived cavalry would strike Meade's rear while Pickett attacked the front. Learning of this plan, Longstreet continued his objections to Lee's offensive strategy. When Lee told him 15,000 men would make the attack, Longstreet replied, "the 15,000 men who could make [a] successful assault over that field" could not be found. Still, Lee pressed on with his plan. Longstreet, however, was becoming increasingly despondent about the idea. He later wrote, "That day at Gettysburg was one of the saddest of my life."

Although Meade had resolved to fight a defensive battle on the third day, he had sent the

BELOW: Breastworks like these on Culp's Hill gave the defenders a huge advantage in the Civil War.

XII Corps back to Culp's Hill to try to regain the ground lost there in previous fighting. At 4:30 a.m. the Federals initiated an artillery bombardment on Major General Edward Johnson's Confederates. Johnson countered by launching an attack of his own at 8:00 a.m. The fighting went back and forth until 11:00 a.m. when a Federal attack forced Johnson to withdraw across Rock Creek. This would be the only contribution Ewell's Corps would make to the fighting on July 3.

Cavalry Battle

The other force Lee had hoped would draw some Federal attention away from the main attack on Cemetery Ridge was that of Stuart's cavalry. Around noon, Stuart deployed some 6,300 men in the woods on Cress's Ridge. Across an open plain to the west were 4,500 Federals. The stage was set for a classic cavalry battle.

After a fight between dismounted troopers in the plain, Stuart launched his 1st Virginia in a charge down the ridge. Traditional cavalry charges with sabers were rare during the Civil War because of the increased effectiveness of infantry defending with rifles. Instead, effective cavalry leaders learned to use their cavalry as mounted infantry. Horses and mules would provide the mobility to get men to the decisive

RIGHT: The 2nd Massachusetts and 27th Indiana Regiments charged across this meadow to dislodge Johnson's Confederates from their positions in the woods.

point, but once there they would dismount and fight. In the Civil War, the dominant weapon of the cavalry was no longer the saber; it was the rifle. Still in this desperate situation, the command "Keep to your sabers, men, keep to your sabers!" went up and down the Confederate ranks.

BELOW: **A countercharge by Brigadier General George Custer and troopers of the Michigan Brigade helped stop the Confederate cavalry.**

Even Federal Brigadier General David Gregg could not help but be impressed by the Confederates' "grand charge," but he counterattacked with the 7th Michigan and stopped the enemy advance. Stuart then committed two columns of squadrons commanded by Brigadier Generals Wade Hampton and Fitzhugh Lee. Federal artillery ripped holes through the depth of this tempting target and then Gregg ordered Brigadier General George Custer forward with the 1st Michigan.

Under pressure from the front and flanks, as well as continued artillery bombardment, the Confederate attack gave way. Custer proudly reported "using the saber only, and driving the enemy from the field." After three hours of fighting, Stuart was forced to retreat to Cress's Ridge, and both sides ended up where they were when the battle began. The Federal cavalry had prevented Stuart from breaking through and diverting forces from the main battle at Cemetery Ridge. The Confederate attack there would be left largely to its own devices.

The Confederates Attack the Center

When Lee heard the fighting in Ewell's sector, he rode to Seminary Ridge where he found Longstreet. Again Longstreet pressed his argument for a turning movement. "General," Longstreet said, "I have had my scouts out all night, and I find that you still have an excellent opportunity to move around to the right of Meade's army, and maneuver him into attacking us." An exasperated Lee pointed to the Federal

EXCERPT FROM STUART'S OFFICIAL REPORT OF THE ACTION ON JULY 3

HDQRS. CAVALRY DIVISION, ARMY OF
NORTHERN VIRGINIA
August 20, 1863

Col. R. H. CHILTON,
Chief of Staff, Army of Northern Virginia

GENERAL: Before General Hampton had reached where I was, the enemy had deployed a heavy line of sharpshooters, and were advancing toward our position, which was very strong. Our artillery had, however, left the crest, which it was essential for it to occupy on account of being of too short range to compete with the longer range guns of the enemy, but I sent orders for its return. Jenkins' brigade was chiefly employed dismounted, and fought with decided effect until the 10 rounds were expended, and then retreated, under circumstances of difficulty and exposure which entailed the loss of valuable men.

The left, where Hampton's and Lee's brigades were, by this time became heavily engaged as dismounted skirmishers. My plan was to employ the enemy in front with sharpshooters, and move a command of cavalry upon their left flank from the position lately held by me, but the falling back of Jenkins' men (that officer was wounded the day previous, before reporting to me, and his brigade was now commanded by Colonel [M. J.] Ferguson, Sixteenth Virginia Cavalry) caused a like movement of those on the left, and the enemy,

sending forward a squadron or two, were about to cut off and capture a portion of our dismounted sharpshooters.

To prevent this, I ordered forward the nearest cavalry regiment (one of W. H. F. Lee's) quickly to charge this force of cavalry. It was gallantly done, and about the same time a portion of General Fitz. Lee's command charged on the left, the First Virginia Cavalry being most conspicuous. ... Their impetuosity carried them too far, and the charge being very much prolonged, their horses, already jaded by hard marching, failed under it. Their movement was too rapid to be stopped by couriers, and the enemy perceiving it, were turning upon them with fresh horses. The First North Carolina Cavalry and Jeff. Davis Legion were sent to their support, and gradually this hand-to-hand fighting involved the greater portion of the command till the enemy were driven from the field, which was now raked by their artillery, posted about three-quarters of a mile off, our officers and men behaving with the greatest heroism throughout. Our own artillery commanding the same ground, no more hand-to-hand fighting occurred, but the wounded were removed and the prisoners (a large number) taken to the rear.

I have the honor to be, most respectfully, your obedient servant,

J. E. B. STUART, Major General.

lines and said, "The enemy is there and I am going to strike him."

In contrast to Longstreet, Pickett relished in the glory of the planned attack. The highlight of Pickett's Mexican-American War service had been carrying the 8th Infantry colors over the ramparts to victory at Chapultepec. Now Pickett was full of optimism and could not help but recall this past glory. When Colonel Birkett Fry, one of Pickett's brigadier generals, reported to work out some details of the attack, he found Pickett "to be in excellent spirits, and after a cordial greeting and a pleasant reference to our having been in work of that kind at Chapultepec, expressed great confidence in the ability of our troops to drive the enemy." Pickett had been wounded at Gaines's Mill during the Peninsula Campaign, and this upcoming battle would be his first fighting command since then. He was as eager for action as Longstreet was reluctant.

By 9:00 a.m., the Confederates were forming in their attack positions in the woods on Seminary Ridge to the west of the Emmitsburg Road. Although the charge is most associated with Pickett's division, his was but one of the units involved. Pickett's division was on the right, Brigadier General James Pettigrew's was on the left, and Major General Isaac Trimble's trailed in support at Pettigrew's right rear.

Pickett concealed his division in the swale in front of Spangler's Woods. Since it would lead the charge, it was well forward of Pettigrew's and Trimble's. From the Federal position on

Cemetery Ridge, the land fell away unevenly and then rose again to the Emmitsburg Road. On either side of the road there was a stout plank and post fence. On the right flank of the Confederate line, there was some 300 yards (275 m) from the road to the ridge. In between was a little swale that offered some cover from enemy fire. On the center and left of the Confederate line the distance from road to ridge was only 135 yards (150 m), but the ground rose almost directly and without cover.

The landmark to guide the Confederate assault was a grove of umbrella-shaped chestnut oaks. Locals called the space Ziegler's Grove but the Confederates described it simply as the "little clump of trees." Perhaps more often in subsequent writings it is referred to as the "copse of trees."

In front of Ziegler's Grove there ran a post and rail fence from south to north along Cemetery Ridge. Behind this fence, stones cleared from the ridge had been piled up to form a crude wall about 2½ to 3 feet (0.75–1 m) high. The wall ran north along the fence until it turned at a right angle just past Ziegler's Grove and ran east for about 80 yards (73 m) before turning north again. The salient created by this course of the wall would become known as the "Angle" in the lore of the battle. Within the Angle, the stone wall was about 2 feet (0.5 m)

FACING PAGE: Wade Hampton was one of Stuart's cavalry brigade commanders at Gettysburg. Here, he fends off Union cavalrymen with his saber.

LEFT: Confederate dead gathered for burial, July 5, 1863.

higher than on the south and north running section below.

Opposing the Confederate main attack were two divisions of Major General Winfield Scott Hancock's II Corps belonging to Major General Alexander Hays and Brigadier General John Gibbon. Hays was at the northern part of the ridge behind the stone wall. At the Angle, Lieutenant Alonzo Cushing and the men of

Battery A, 4th U.S. Artillery stood with six 3-inch (76 mm) ordnance rifles. They were supported by Brigadier General Alexander Webb's Philadelphia Brigade. Gibbon's division picked up the line to the south, but by then the stone wall had run its course. The men in this sector were protected only by a hastily erected earthwork about knee high.

The Role of Artillery

The Confederate assault was to be preceded by a massive artillery bombardment. Ostensibly, responsibility for planning this phase of the attack rested with Lee's Chief of Artillery, Brigadier General William Pendleton. Although a West Point graduate, Pendleton had soon left the military and pursued the life of an Episcopalian minister. Now, according to one frustrated Confederate, "Pendleton is Lee's weakness. He is like the elephant, we have him and don't know what on earth to do with him, and it costs a devil of a sight to feed him." Brigadier General Moxley Sorrel, Longstreet's observant chief of staff, described Pendleton as "a well-meaning man without qualities for the high post he claimed—Chief of the Artillery of the Army." At Gettysburg, Pendleton reported to have given his "earnest attention" to the myriad tasks associated with planning the bombardment. In

BELOW: Major General Winfield Scott Hancock's II Corps bore the brunt of the Confederate attack on July 3.

FACING PAGE: Frontal attacks in the Mexican War, such as the one George Pickett participated in at Chapultepec, were much more likely to succeed than those conducted during the Civil War.

reality, the responsibility fell to Colonel Edward Porter Alexander, Longstreet's artillery chief.

Not yet 30 years old, Alexander had an energy and sense of urgency that Pendleton lacked. He had a diverse background, having served early in his career as an engineer and then as one of the pioneers of the "wigwag" signal communications system. He had even made several ascents in observation balloons during the Peninsula Campaign. His career as an artillerist began formally in November 1862 when he became commander of an artillery battalion under Longstreet and distinguished himself at Fredericksburg where he positioned his guns at Marye's Heights. From the commanding position, Alexander correctly predicted that "a chicken could not live on that field when we open on it." He began the Gettysburg Campaign in command of one of Longstreet's artillery reserve battalions, but during the battle Longstreet put Alexander in tactical command of the corps' artillery. The move bypassed Longstreet's erstwhile Chief of Artillery, Colonel James Walton and certainly upset Walton, but Longstreet recognized Alexander was the best man for the job.

There was much to make Alexander's task a difficult one. During the Mexican-American War, artillery had often been used in an offensive role, pounding the enemy's guns and infantry at relatively short range to create a breach in the enemy's defenses through which the friendly infantry could pass. This technique was possible because of artillery's advantage in "stand-off," meaning that the artillery had a greater range than the infantry muskets opposing it. With such a differential in their favor, Mexican-American War artillerists were able to leisurely work their guns without much fear of infantry muskets endangering them.

BELOW: Much of the Confederate artillery barrage had landed long and did not appreciably degrade the Federal defenses along Cemetery Ridge.

FACING PAGE: This bird's-eye view of the Gettysburg battlefield clearly shows the town's importance as a junction of several roads as well as the famous fish-hook shape of the Federal lines.

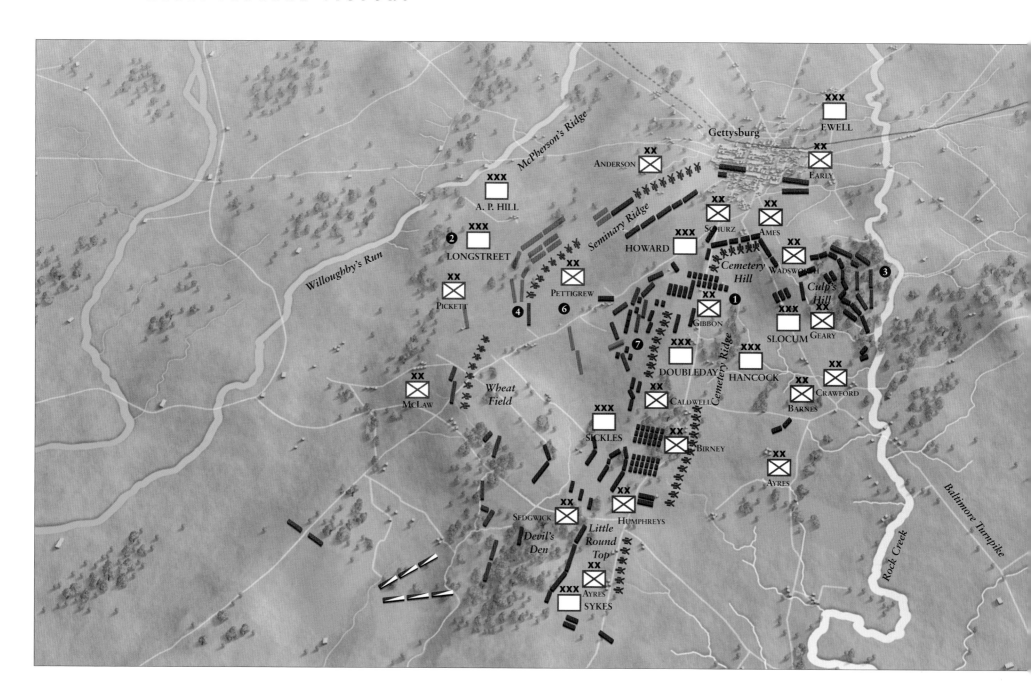

McPherson's Ridge

Willoughby's Run

Gettysburg

ANDERSON

XXX
A. P. HILL

XXX
LONGSTREET

❷

Seminary Ridge

XX
PICKETT

XXX
EWELL

XX
EARLY

XX
SCHURZ

XX
AMES

XXX
HOWARD

Cemetery Hill

XX
WADSWORTH

Culp's Hill

❸

XX
PETTIGREW

❹   ❻

XX
GIBBON

❶

XXX
SLOCUM

XX
GEARY

❼

XXX
DOUBLEDAY

Cemetery Ridge

XXX
HANCOCK

XX
CRAWFORD

XX
McLAW

Wheat Field

XX
CALDWELL

XX
BARNES

XXX
SICKLES

XX
BIRNEY

XX
AYRES

XX
SEDGWICK

Devil's Den

XX
HUMPHREYS

Little Round Top

XX
AYRES

XXX
SYKES

Rock Creek

Baltimore Turnpike

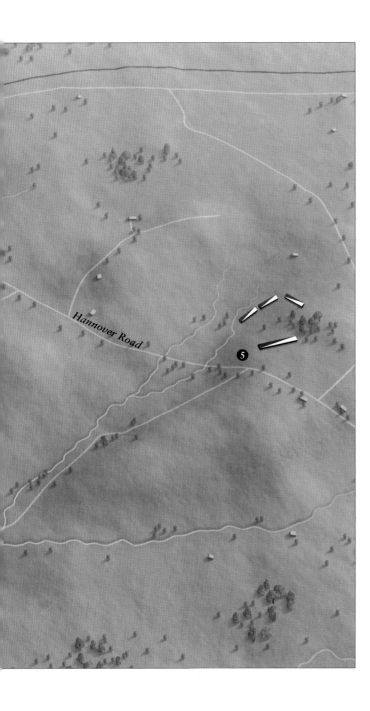

PHASE THREE
July 3

❶ At the end of the second day's fighting, Meade correctly warned Gibbon that if Lee attacked again it would be in the Federal center.
❷ Although Longstreet was in command of the attack, he was so pessimistic of its success that he did little to influence the action.
❸ At 4:30 a.m., Meade began an artillery bombardment at Culp's Hill. At 8:00 a.m., Johnson launched an inconsequential counterattack. Ewell's Corps did little else in the ensuing battle.
❹ Alexander opened a pre-assault bombardment at 1:00 p.m. It failed to have the desired effect on the Federal line.
❺ At about the same time as Alexander began his artillery bombardment, Stuart launched an unsuccessful cavalry charge against the Federal rear. The attack was beaten back by Federal cavalry.
❻ At about 2:00 p.m., after Alexander assessed his artillery had reached its maximum effect, "Pickett's Charge" began.
❼ Orienting on the "copse of trees," the Confederate attack reached its "High Water Mark," before being repulsed at the stone wall in front of Cushing's battery.

By the time of the Civil War, this relationship would change because of the popular use of greater ranged rifles by the infantry, giving a great advantage to the defender. Against protected defenders, the artillery could not get close enough to have the desired effect with canister without exposing the gunners to the long range fires of the defenders' rifles. Although rifled artillery had also been developed and provided greater range and accuracy, it proved somewhat less reliable and slower to load than smoothbores. Furthermore, the increased range of cannons provided no real advantage in the broken and wooded terrain common on so many Civil War battlefields.

Defensive Role

The result was that most successful Civil War artillery actions would be defensive rather than offensive. The Army of Northern Virginia had experienced this painful truth at Malvern Hill on July 1, 1862. Nonetheless, Lee had hoped to, at the close of the preliminary bombardment, push batteries forward along with the advancing infantry to provide close-in fires.

In addition to the tactical problems associated with the offensive use of artillery, the Confederate cannoneers were plagued by faulty ammunition and fuses. The result was often shells that either failed to burst or did so prematurely. Coordinating artillery fires with infantry movements under such circumstances was difficult and dangerous. As Alexander explained, "We were always liable to premature

FACING PAGE: The Army of Northern Virginia knew the fearful costs of attacking into the face of Federal artillery from the Battle of Malvern Hill in 1862.

explosions of shell & shrapnel, & our infantry knew it by sad experience, & I have known of their threatening to fire back at our guns if we opened over their heads."

The final problem facing Alexander was a shortage of ammunition. After a three-week campaign, the Army of Northern Virginia had exhausted much of its ammunition and had no hope of gaining fresh supplies unless they were captured from the enemy. Apparently Pendleton had not kept good accounts of how much ammunition was on hand so it was impossible to determine whether or not there was a sufficient quantity available for an effective bombardment and continued support of the assault. Lee was unaware of the critical shortage of ammunition, and after the war several commentators including Major General Lafayette McLaws argued that had Lee known the disappointing reality, he would not have ordered Pickett's Charge.

Early Assault

Lee's initial plan was for an early morning assault, so Alexander was up before dawn trying to get his guns in position. He was alarmed to find many pieces dangerously close to the Federal batteries, and by quiet and fast work he was able to pull them to safer positions. He then began forming his line. He placed 75 guns from

LEFT: A monument marks where the batteries of Alexander's Battalion, a part of Longstreet's Corps, fought on July 2 and July 3. The plaque includes details of the guns employed, including Parrott guns, 3-inch (76mm) Napoleons, and 24 pounder howitzers.

EXCERPT FROM "AN HOUR AND FORTY MINUTES," A LETTER TO THE *NEW YORK TIMES*, JULY 6, 1863

In the shadow cast by the tiny farmhouse, sixteen by twenty, which General Meade had made his headquarters, lay wearied staff officers and tired journalists. There was not wanting to the peacefulness of the scene the singing of a bird, which had a nest in a peach tree within the tiny yard of the whitewashed cottage. In the midst of its warbling, a shell screamed over the house, instantly followed by another, and another, and in a moment the air was full of the most complete artillery prelude to an infantry battle that was ever exhibited. Every size and form of shell known to British and to American gunnery, shrieked, whirled, moaned, whistled, and wrathfully fluttered over our ground. As many as six in a second, constantly two in a second, bursting and screaming over and around headquarters, made a very hell of fire that amazed the oldest officers. They burst in the yard—burst next to the fence on both sides, garnished as usual with the hitched horses of aids and orderlies. The fastened animals reared and plunged with terror. Then one fell, then another—sixteen lay dead and mangled before the fire ceased. Still fastened by their halters, which gave the impression of their being wickedly tied up to die painfully, these brute victims of a cruel war touched all hearts. … A shell tore up the little step of the headquarters cottage, and ripped bags of oats as with a knife. Soon a spherical came opposite the open door—

another ripped through the low garret. The remaining pillar went almost immediately to the howl of a fixed shot that Whitworth must have made. During this fire, the horses at twenty and thirty feet distant were receiving their death, and soldiers in Federal blue were torn to pieces in the road, and died with the peculiar yells that blend the extorted cry of pain with horror and despair. Not an orderly—not an ambulance—not a straggler was to be seen upon the plain swept by this tempest of orchestral death, thirty minutes after it commenced. Were not one hundred and fifty pieces of artillery trying to cut from the field every battery we had in position to resist their purposed infantry attack, and sweep away the slight defences behind which our infantry were waiting? Forty minutes—fifty minutes—counted on watches that ran, O, so languidly! Shells through the two lower rooms! A shell into the chimney that fortunately did not explode. Shells in the yard. The air thicker and fuller, and more deafening with the howling and whirling of these infernal missiles. The chief of staff struck. Seth Williams, loved and respected through the army, separated from instant death by two inches of space vertically measured. An aid bored with a fragment of iron through the bone of the arm. Another cut with an exploded piece of case shot. And the time measured on the sluggish watches was one hour and forty minutes.

Longstreet's I Corps along a front extending 1,300 yards (1,200 m) from the Peach Orchard northward behind the Emmitsburg Road to Spangler's Woods. He guarded his southern flank with eight other guns to ward off attacking infantry. Several hundred yards to the left and rear of his main line, Alexander had 60 guns from Hill's III Corps. Past them were 24 guns from Ewell's II Corps. All told, Alexander had about 170 guns with an average of 130 to 150 rounds each.

As Alexander prepared for the pre-assault bombardment, he received a note from Longstreet asking Alexander to determine whether or not the artillery had done enough damage to make the attack viable. In a gesture indicative of his reluctance for the task at hand, Longstreet asked, "If the artillery fire does not have the effect to drive off the enemy or greatly demoralize him so as to make our effort pretty certain I would prefer that you should not advise Gen Pickett to make the charge. I shall rely a great deal upon your good judgment to determine the matter, and shall expect you to let Gen Pickett know when the moment offers."

It was a thinly disguised effort to shift the responsibility to the young Alexander who replied that he would not be able to assess the results to

FACING PAGE: This contemporary magazine illustration shows Confederate artillery firing at Cemetery Hill, the gates to the cemetery clearly visible. In spite of Alexander's best efforts, the Confederate artillery was outmatched at Gettysburg.

that degree of accuracy. "I will only be able to judge the effect of our fire on the enemy by his return fire as his infantry is but little exposed to view & the smoke will obscure the whole field," replied Alexander. "If as I infer from your note there is any alternative to this attack it should be carefully considered before opening our fire, for it will take all the arty ammunition we have left to test this one thoroughly & if the result is unfavorable we will have none left for another effort & even if this is entirely successful it can only be so at a very bloody cost."

Longstreet then sent Alexander a second note that largely restated the first one. "Colonel," Longstreet began. "The intention is to advance the infantry if the artillery has the desired effect of driving the enemy's off, or having other effect such as to warrant us making the attack." Then, refusing to relieve Alexander of the momentous decision, Longstreet added, "When the moment arrives advise Gen. Pickett and of course advance such artillery as you can use in aiding the attack." An incredulous Brigadier General Ambrose Wright, who was at the time with Alexander, told him, "He has put the responsibility back upon you."

Alexander knew he had no means of making such an assessment. He later wrote "whether or not that attack was to be made, must be decided before the cannonade opened." Unable to judge the effect on the enemy, the best Alexander could

RIGHT: "Hancock the Superb" created a powerful command presence wherever he went.

do was report on his own fires. "When our fire is at its best," he wrote Longstreet, "I will advise Gen. Pickett to advance."

Opening Barrage

Alexander began his bombardment at 1:00 p.m. It was a ferocious cannonade, but most of the rounds—as many as 90 percent according to one no doubt exaggerating officer—sailed over the heads of the Federal positions on Cemetery Ridge. Thus, some of the most vulnerable personnel were the camp followers, teamsters, ambulance drivers, and wounded in the field hospitals who thought they were out of harm's way. The Leister house, where Meade had made his headquarters some 400 yards (365 m) behind the center of the main line, was among the hardest hit areas.

In spite of the hail of shell, Hancock rode the length of the II Corps line with an orderly carrying the corps colors behind him. His calm display brought cheers from his men. When a staff officer admonished Hancock for exposing himself so, Hancock replied, "There are times when a corps commander's life does not count."

Knowing an infantry charge would follow the Confederate bombardment, Hunt had ordered the Federal artillery to hold its fire for some 15 minutes in an effort to conserve ammunition. Hunt had not briefed Hancock on this plan, and Hancock was enraged that the Federal guns were silent. Among other things, Hancock was worried that the unanswered bombardment would demoralize his infantry. He ordered

Captain John Hazard, the II Corps chief of artillery, to commence firing. Hazard responded with the five batteries belonging to II Corps, but further south Lieutenant Colonel Freeman McGilvery kept his 41 guns of the reserve artillery quiet in obedience to Hunt's order.

BELOW: Stephen Vincent Benet immortalized Alonzo Cushing in the verse, "He held his guts in his hand as the charge came up the wall. And his gun spoke out for him once before he fell to the ground."

Hancock demanded McGilvery fire, but McGilvery held his ground—an important show of will that kept McGilvery's position undetected and his ammunition available when the Confederates did finally charge.

While much of the Confederate fire sailed overhead, some rounds found their mark.

Among the heaviest hit locations was Cushing's battery, and infantrymen had to be called forward to replace the wounded artillerymen. The infantrymen also soon became casualties. One was wounded so terribly he begged someone to put him out of his misery. When no one would, he pulled out his pistol and ended

BELOW: Alonzo Cushing and his artillery at Little Round Top. Cushing's battery was among the cast of Federal heroes on July 3.

his own life. Cushing, too, was wounded in the shoulder and groin. Refusing calls for him to go to the rear, Cushing said, "No, I stay right here and fight it out or die in the attempt." For his heroic action, Brevet Major Alonzo Cushing was approved by the U.S. Congress to receive the Medal of Honor in 2010. The announcement was made almost 150 years after Gettysburg.

During the bombardment, Hunt rode the line to check on his batteries. He finally reached Evergreen Cemetery on Cemetery Hill where he met XI Corps commander Howard and his artillery chief, Major Thomas Osborn. By now most observers had concluded the Confederates were planning to assault the Federal center. Osborn reported that Meade had recently visited and "expressed the hope that the enemy would attack, and he had no fear of the result."

To encourage this outcome, Osborn suggested holding the Federal fire to trick Lee into thinking his bombardment had been successful. Hunt liked the idea and soon learned Meade did too. Hunt passed the word to his batteries to hold their fire, and then he ordered four fresh batteries from the artillery reserve to reinforce the center of the Federal line. Meade was also moving infantry reinforcements forward. When the Confederates charged, the Federals would be ready.

Alexander had not yet noticed a significant reduction in the enemy fire, but he did know his own guns were quickly running out of ammunition. About half an hour later, he sent Pickett a note, telling him that now was the best time to attack. "General," he wrote. "If you are

A LETTER FROM CORPORAL ALFRED CARPENTER, COMPANY K, 1st MINNESOTA REGIMENT

Warrenton Junction, VA
July 30, 1863

We roused before day, but late in the morning, July 3rd, everything was quiet as death along the whole line, but not even the private soldier was deceived, he knew it presaged a storm which at last broke upon us with all its fury. We lay behind a ridge of land about three feet in height. All at once the guns opened and from morn till middle of afternoon it raged with terrific violence. Flat upon the ground we lay, while the vertical rays of the July sun rendered the heat almost intolerable. To rise up was almost certain death, while flat upon the ground we were tolerable well protected. If the shots went high enough to go above the ridge they went over us; if they struck the ridge, they ricocheted over our prostrate bodies though uncomfortably near and occasionally falling among us.

The Rebels could not injure us much except by bursting shells in the air in front of us, and as their object was to silence our batteries they did us little damage, though shot and shell flew over us in such rapid succession that it was impossible to count them, and very near to our bodies at times, one shell actually tearing the knap sack from a man's back as he lay face downward. There were over two hundred guns at work in this part of the line, firing as fast as men could load them. The noise it produced, the whistling of solid shot; the screeching of shells; the bursting of spherical case; the explosion of caissons, the roar of the pieces is indescribable. I can think of no adjective or collection of adjectives that will describe it. It must be seen, heard, felt, to be understood. How a wounded man attempts to go back to a hospital and perhaps is cut down before he can go in the rear of the ridge fifteen rods behind us. A case of sun-stroke and his comrades start to carry him off; perhaps one of their number is looped off; perhaps all pass uninjured. By turning on our backs we can see our artillery. It is getting roughly handled. A dozen of our caissons have already exploded. Gun after gun is dismounted by the solid shots of the enemy.

A. P. Carpenter

to advance at all, you must come at once or we will not be able to support you as we ought. But the enemy's fire has not slackened materially and there are still eighteen guns firing from the cemetery."

BELOW: Longstreet gives orders to Pickett for his division to charge the Federal positions. Longstreet held little hope for Pickett's Charge.

Soon after sending the note, Alexander began to "notice some of the enemy's guns ceasing to fire." Seeing some guns moving to the rear without replacement, he "felt encouraged to believe that they had felt very severe punishment, & that my fire had been generally well aimed & as effective as could be hoped." About 15 minutes after sending the first note, Alexander sent Pickett another: "For God's sake come quick. The eighteen guns are gone. Come quick or my ammunition will not let me support you properly."

Pickett's Charge

Pickett rode to Longstreet and excitedly asked, "General, shall I advance?" The reluctant Longstreet could not bring himself to do more than merely nod his head. With that unenthusiastic gesture, Pickett was off.

When the assault began, the Confederate line measured about a mile (1.6 km) from left to right. The ground was crisscrossed by shallow depressions that provided only temporary cover, and the attackers were exposed to the galling fire of the Federal batteries from Little Round Top to Cemetery Hill. Large gaps were punched in the Confederate ranks, but after 15 minutes the attackers reached the Emmitsburg Road and dressed their lines. By now the Federal artillery was blasting the Confederates with canister within 400 yards (365 m), creating more holes. The Confederates consolidated their lines, shrinking their front to just a half mile (0.8 km) from flank to flank.

Pettigrew's division was at best marginally led. Pettigrew had only been in command a matter of days, replacing a wounded Heth. Colonel James Marshall then assumed command of Pettigrew's old brigade. Colonel Fry was also new to brigade command, filling in for Brigadier General James Archer who had been captured earlier. Brigadier General Joseph Davis had been in brigade command for a while but his background was in law and many attributed his position to the fact that he was President Jefferson Davis's nephew rather than to any military skills. Colonel John Brockenbrough, who had been tepid in the first two days' fighting, had now inexplicably split his brigade into two halves. He took charge of two regiments and turned the other two over to Colonel Robert Mayo. To make matters worse, III Corps commander Hill chose to provide Pettigrew little guidance as he prepared for the climactic action.

The inadequacies of this organization quickly became apparent. Fry's brigade was Pettigrew's right-hand unit and the one on which Pickett would guide. Fry moved out without hesitation, confessing that "after lying inactive under that deadly storm of hissing and exploding shells it seemed a relief to go forward to the desperate assault." Marshall, on Fry's left, also advanced, but Davis somehow did not see Marshall move and got off to a late start. As the men hurried to catch up, Davis failed to keep them in proper formation and they bunched up, presenting an easy target for the Federals. Things got worse on

the far left with Brockenbrough. Pettigrew expected little of that brigade and when it failed to move he sent a staff officer to check on it, telling him it might attack but "if it failed to do so it would not matter." Indeed once Brockenbrough's divided command got moving, it soon halted when it came under enemy fire. As Brockenbrough drifted off into irrelevance,

the rest of Pettigrew's division pressed on to the Emmitsburg Road. There they were within 400 yards (365 yards) of Hays's defenders, and Federal artillery blasted the Confederates with canister. Hays had concentrated his defense, packing as many men as he could behind the stone wall. The Federal fire was intense and the results devastating. Fry was wounded in the

ABOVE: For many, the Confederate soldiers of Pickett's Charge epitomized bravery, glory, and duty as they advanced toward the Federal positions.

FACING PAGE: Isaac Trimble led the trail division in Pickett's Charge and was wounded in the attack.

thigh and had to be carried from the field. Marshall was shot in the head and killed. With Brockenbrough absent on his flank, Davis was hit hard by enfilading fire from the 8th Ohio forward of the road.

Brigadier General Isaac Trimble, advancing to the right rear of Pettigrew's division, watched as the attack disintegrated around the Emmitsburg Road. Soon Pettigrew sent word asking Trimble to move forward to shore up the crumbling flank. Confusion followed, but Brigadier General James Lane got three and a half of his five regiments forward, only to be halted by a murderous fire from the front and flank. Trimble then sent Colonel William Lowrance's understrength brigade forward. It fared little better than Lane's, and Hays's line held strong.

Turning the Attack

After Pickett crossed the Emmitsburg Road, he had to oblique to the left to close the gap between his division and Pettigrew's. This 45-degree turn took Pickett's men right across the front of Gibbon's division. Brigadier General James Kemper's brigade on the Confederate right was the first to feel the effects of the raking Federal fire. Of particular notice were the 36 guns of Lieutenant Colonel McGilvery positioned on the southern end of Cemetery Ridge. One of McGilvery's officers reported,

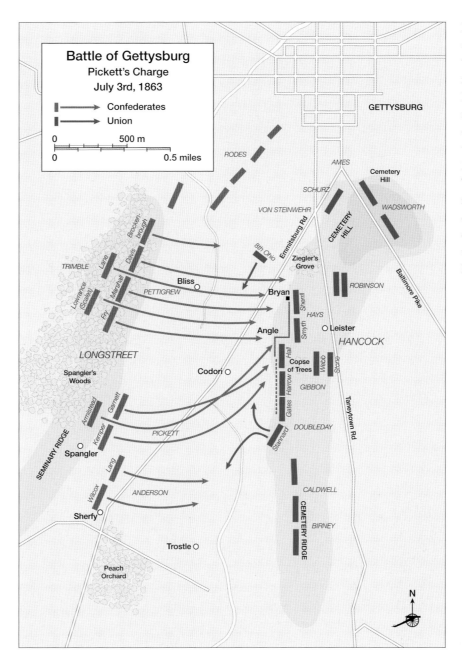

LEFT: Although often described as "Pickett's Charge," Pickett's was the lead division of three, including Trimble's and Pettigrew's. Pickett's men were mostly from Virginia, with the other divisions consisting of troops from North Carolina, Mississippi, Alabama, and Tennessee. The 12,500 men marched deliberately in line, charging only when close to the enemy. The nine brigades made up a front of over a mile (1.6 km) long.

EXCERPT FROM A LETTER FROM CORPORAL ALFRED CARPENTER , COMPANY K, 1st MINNESOTA REGIMENT

Warrenton Junction, VA
July 30, 1863

For two hours we had fought desperately. The men seemed inspired and fought with a determination unconquerable. I believe they would have died or taken on the spot before yielding. Men fell about us unheeded, unnoticed; we scarcely knew they were falling, so great was the intensity of attention to approaching foe. Our muskets became so heated we could no longer handle them. We dropped them and picked up those of the wounded. Our cartridges gave out. We rifled the boxes of the dead. Artillerymen from the disabled pieces in our rear sprang forward, and seizing guns and cartridges from the wounded, fought by our side as infantrymen. Many of the men became deaf, and did not recover their hearing for a day or two. It was a grand and terrible scene. I wish I could paint it to you as I was and felt it.

A. P. Carpenter

BELOW: Lewis Armistead was a Mexican War veteran and old army friend of Winfield Scott Hancock.

"We could not help hitting them at every shot." Two regiments of Brigadier General George Stannard's Vermont brigade also poured fire into Kemper's right flank. The Confederates drifted left to try to distance themselves from the fire, and when Kemper tried to redirect them he was severely wounded by a bullet near his spine.

Brigadier General Richard Garnett's brigade was on the left of Pickett's division. As Kemper's brigade pushed left into Garnett's, Garnett rode up and down the line trying to restore order. He personally advanced within 20 yards (18 m) of the Federal lines and disappeared into the smoke and confusion. Moments later, his riderless horse, streaming with blood, galloped to the rear. Garnett, presumably unidentified as a general and buried by the Federals in a common trench, was never seen again.

With the Confederate right and left flanks broken, only the center remained. The attack there consisted of a brigade of five Virginia regiments led by Brigadier General Lewis Armistead. Their objective was the stone wall that protected Cushing and his guns. Armistead led his brigade forward, orienting on Ziegler's Grove and cheering his men on with his hat on his sword.

As the Confederates surged forward, they were met by Federal reinforcements who were

FACING PAGE: Presenting a conspicuous target on his horse, Richard Garnett was killed during Pickett's Charge and his body not recovered.

also rushing toward the stone wall. Gibbon had earlier sent Lieutenant Frank Haskell to report to Meade and when Haskell returned he could not find Gibbon or Hancock. Quickly assessing the situation, Haskell found Colonel Norman Hall, one of Gibbon's brigade commanders. "Webb is hotly pressed," Haskell explained, "and must have support or he will be overpowered. Can you assist him?"

As Hall was shifting his forces to the right, Haskell rode to Colonel William Harrow who commanded the 1st Minnesota that had fought so bravely but been severely bloodied the day before. Harrow rushed his men to the fight. A general melee ensued.

At one point, 150 Confederates poured over the wall and momentarily broke the Federal line, but the defenders recovered, rushed forward fresh artillery, and opened fire less than 10 yards (9 m) from Armistead and his men. As Federals closed in from all sides, Armistead reached a captured Federal cannon, put his hand on it, and was shot. However, having come this far, the isolated Confederates could not sustain their attack. Today, a small monument bearing the

FACING PAGE: The 69th Pennsylvania defended forward of the copse of trees that provided focus for the Confederate attack.

RIGHT: This painting shows the Confederate soldiers who broke through the wall, briefly penetrating the Federal line. Rail fences were among the obstacles that made the Confederate battle line hard to control.

BELOW: *Repulse of Longstreet's Assault,* by John C. Bachelder, circa 1876. The original caption reads: "In the left foreground, you can see Union soldiers tending to the mortally wounded General Armistead. The Angle and the Copse of Trees are immediately above his head. To the right of the two trees at the Angle are the burning buildings of the Bliss Farm. Further to the right are the barn and small home of the Abraham Bryan Farm."

inscription "High Water Mark of the Rebellion" marks the spot where the Confederate attack finally was repulsed.

Armistead and Hancock were dear friends, and the coincidence that they would face each other at the climactic point of the Gettysburg battlefield is often used to epitomize the pathos of old army comrades now fighting each other as enemies. In a different time, they had

stormed Chapultepec together with the 6th Infantry in the Mexican-American War. Later, when the eve of the Civil War found many Southerners like Armistead on duty in the west, they gathered in Los Angeles, seeking transportation back to their native states. Hancock was serving there as a quartermaster, and on June 15, 1861, he hosted a farewell party for his friends as they departed for their

separate sides in the Civil War. Armistead was emotionally torn by the situation, telling Hancock, "You can never know what this has cost me, and I hope God will strike me dead if I am ever induced to leave my native soil, should worst come to worst." Then Armistead entrusted Mrs. Hancock with a small satchel of personal items and mementos to be opened only in the event Armistead was killed.

Now at Gettysburg, the wounded Armistead was taken prisoner, and, as the life slipped away from him, he asked that his captors deliver a message to his old friend Hancock. Accounts vary, but Armistead reportedly said words to the effect of "Tell General Hancock for me that I have done him and done you all an injury which I shall regret the longest day I live." The exact meaning of Armistead's words has been much debated, but at least one conclusion is that Armistead had learned that Hancock had also been wounded, and Armistead was filled with grief by the part he had played in harming his old friend.

ABOVE: Today, a memorial marks what has been popularly termed the "High Water Mark of the Confederacy."

FACING PAGE: This lithograph produced in the 1880s shows Pickett's Charge. Henry Hunt's well-placed artillery was instrumental in successfully repulsing the Confederate assault.

"How is it going here?"

Meade reached the crest of the ridge too late to witness the dramatic climax of Pickett's Charge. When he did arrive, he asked the indefatigable Haskell, "How is it going here?" "I believe, General, the enemy's attack is repulsed," said Haskell. "What! Is the assault entirely repulsed?" exclaimed Meade. "It is, Sir," said Haskell, to which Meade replied, "Thank God!" It is fitting that Haskell would have the honor of delivering the good news to Meade. There was no shortage of heroes at Gettysburg, but Gibbon felt Haskell "did more than any one man to repulse that last assault at Gettysburg, and he did the part of a general there."

The results of Pickett's Charge were a powerful testimony to the impact of modern weapons and the futility of frontal assaults across open terrain. In previous wars such as in Mexico, the offense had many advantages over the defense. By the time of the Civil War, technological developments had reversed this relationship.

In 1853, the U.S. Army had adopted the rifled infantry musket. By this time, a French Army captain named Claude E. Minie had developed a way to load a rifled musket as easily as a smoothbore. The "Minie ball" was a cylindro-conoidal bullet that was slightly smaller in diameter than the barrel and thus could be easily dropped down the barrel. One end, however, was hollow, and, when the rifle was fired, expanding gas widened the sides of this hollow end so that the bullet would grip the rifling and create the spinning effect needed for accuracy. To take advantage of this technology, the United States adapted the Model 1855 Springfield rifle to take .58 caliber Minie ammunition. The difference was significant. The smoothbore musket had a range of 100 to 200 yards (90–180 m). The new rifle was effective from 400 to 600 yards (350–550 m).

However, this change in technology was not accompanied by a drastic change in tactics. Civil War formations remained fixed in the old Napoleonic style with men standing shoulder to shoulder and small intervals between units. The lines were maintained rigidly parallel to allow for a massed or uniform volley at the halt and to maximize the shock effect. Commanders knew such a formation presented a vulnerable target, but they felt that an attack coming in successive waves would eventually overwhelm the defenders and carry the field.

In actuality, frontal attacks such as Pickett's Charge proved deadly. Nearly 5,600 men, over 50 percent of the Confederates who had made the charge became casualties. As a demonstration of the disproportionate strength of the defense, Federal casualties were only about 1,500. One Confederate survivor wrote, "It was a second Fredericksburg... only the wrong way."

BELOW: This monument marks the spot where Armistead fell mortally wounded.

The Confederate Withdrawal

As difficult as it must have been, Lee now had to ready his shattered army for the possibility of a counterattack. He saw Pickett and rode over to meet him. "General Pickett," Lee said, "place your division in rear of this hill, and be ready to repel the advance of the enemy should they follow up their advantage." A despondent Pickett cried, "General Lee, I have no division now, Armistead is down, Garnett is down, and Kemper is mortally wounded." "Come, General Pickett," replied Lee, "this has been my fight and upon my shoulders rests the blame. The men and officers of your command have written the name of Virginia as high today as it has ever been written before."

Other of Lee's lieutenants followed including a gravely wounded Kemper. Kemper lifted himself up on his litter and asked Lee to "do full justice to this division for its work today." Lee bowed his head and said, "I will" as the men carried Kemper away. To every one of his men he saw, Lee offered some word of comfort, cheer, or exhortation.

The Confederates had taken some prisoners along the Emmitsburg Road, and Lee passed one wounded Federal who defiantly shouted, "Hurrah for the Union." Lee stopped his horse Traveller, dismounted, and approached the man, who no doubt feared now for his life. Instead,

FACING PAGE: Confederate prisoners being marched away. Many of the Confederates captured at Gettysburg were sent to Fort Delaware as prisoners.

Lee extended his hand and said, "My son, I hope you will soon be well."

But even in victory, Meade's army had been badly bruised, and the counterattack Lee feared never materialized. Still Lee knew his own casualties were too high and his supplies too

BELOW: The Confederate flag shown here is the "Stars and Bars," often confused with the more well-known Confederate battle flag.

low for him to remain in Northern territory. "We must now return to Virginia," Lee concluded, and he began issuing orders for the retreat.

A key part in the withdrawal would be played by Brigadier General John Imboden and his cavalry brigade, which had not reached Gettysburg until noon on July 3. Imboden waited at Lee's headquarters until 1:00 a.m. when Lee finally arrived, "riding alone, at a slow walk, and evidently wrapped in profound thought." Imboden wrote Lee bore "an expression of sadness I had never seen before upon his face." Awkwardly, Imboden said, "General, this has been a hard day on you." "Yes," replied Lee, "it has been a sad, sad day to us." After a moment or two of silence, Lee revived and exclaimed, "I never saw troops behave more magnificently than Pickett's division of Virginians did today in that grand charge upon the enemy. And if they had been supported as they were to have been—but for some reason not yet fully explained to me, were not—we would have held the position and the day would have been ours." After another brief pause, Lee sighed with regret, "Too bad. Oh! Too bad."

Having allowed himself this short period of retrospection, Lee recovered himself and assigned Imboden the difficult task of escorting the army's wounded and most of its supply wagons back to Virginia. Fitzhugh Lee's and Wade Hampton's cavalry would guard the flanks and rear. Imboden's column left the next

EXCERPT FROM *THREE MONTHS IN THE SOUTHERN STATES* BY ARTHUR FREMANTLE (A BRITISH OBSERVER TRAVELING WITH LEE'S ARMY)

July 3, 1863

I saw General Wilcox (an officer who wears a short round jacket and a battered straw hat) come up to [Lee], and explain, almost crying, the state of his brigade. General Lee immediately shook hands with him and said cheerfully, "Never mind, General, all this has been my fault—it is I that have lost this fight, and you must help me out of it in the best way you can." In this manner I saw General Lee encourage and reanimate his somewhat dispirited troops, and magnanimously take upon his own shoulders the whole weight of the repulse. It was impossible to look at him or to listen to him without feeling the strongest admiration . ...

day at 4:00 p.m. on what would be a tortuous 17-mile (27 km) trek northwest across the South Mountain to Chambersburg, then south to Hagerstown, and on to Williamsport to a ford and pontoon bridge across the Potomac.

It must have been with a heavy heart that Lee issued the retreat order, and Gettysburg was clearly the low point of his career. The initial decision to invade the North now seemed ill-advised, and based largely on Lee's

overconfidence in his men and underestimation of his enemy. Especially on the heels of the great victory at Chancellorsville, Lee was convinced that the Army of Northern Virginia could win by attacking. Outnumbered and forfeiting to Meade the defender's advantage, Lee's offensive strategy, however, was a dangerously risky one.

Longstreet had hoped to minimize these risks by urging Lee to combine the strategic offensive with defensive tactics. Longstreet had made his case in the campaign's initial planning stages, but even after July 1, Lee still had alternatives that were in keeping with Longstreet's ideas. Lee could have withdrawn southward, taking all the supplies he had gathered with him, and accomplished his important objective of providing relief to war-torn Virginia. Lee, however, continued to seek victory through decisive battle. Steeped in the Napoleonic tradition, Lee sought a strategy of annihilation that was simply beyond the capability of the Confederacy's limited resources to obtain.

Jennie Wade

The southern end of the town of Gettysburg continually found itself caught in the crossfire from Federal and Confederate skirmishers. Twenty-year old Jennie (sometimes Ginnie) Wade became the only civilian fatality during the Battle of Gettysburg when a stray Confederate bullet struck her while she was in her kitchen. A seamstress by trade, Jennie and her family fled to her sister, Georgia Wade McClellan's, home

LEFT: The house in which Jennie Wade was killed has become a popular site for Gettysburg tourists.

BELOW: Jennie Wade's sweetheart, Corporal Johnston Skelly, was wounded near Winchester, Virginia and died on July 12 without ever knowing of Jennie's fate.

on Baltimore Street on July 1. Georgia's husband was away in the Federal Army, and Jennie was helping care for her sister's young children. She also spent the first two days of the battle baking and distributing bread to Federal soldiers and filling their canteens with water. She was kneading dough for biscuits when she was struck by a bullet and killed instantly on July 3. A monument marks her grave in Evergreen Cemetery.

Command and Control

An equally important criticism of Lee's generalship at Gettysburg is his failure to

LEFT: **This map shows the battle as it unfolded on July 3. Meade had correctly predicted that Lee's attack would strike the center of the Federal line.**

supervise effectively his lieutenants. While working with Stonewall Jackson, Lee was able to give the broad discretionary orders with which he was comfortable, but Lee did not have this luxury with his other corps commanders, and he failed to adjust his leadership style accordingly. His vague order to Ewell to take Cemetery Hill "if practicable" on the first day of the battle is the prime example. Jackson would have understood Lee wanted that key terrain secured and would have acted accordingly. Ewell did not interpret the order in the same way and elected to not pursue the opportunity.

Lee's dealings with Longstreet also showed a lack of proper supervision. Lee knew Longstreet had reservations about the entire offensive and specifically about continuing the battle the second day. Nonetheless, Lee did nothing to ensure Longstreet acted aggressively, and the result was an unacceptably slow initiation of the attack. With Jackson, Lee could reason and persuade, but with Longstreet, Lee had to be firm and resolute. While Longstreet obeyed Lee's orders, he did so grudgingly and without enthusiasm. Lee failed to bring his subordinate's will in line with his own.

Finally, Lee failed to control his cavalryman Jeb Stuart. By this point in the war, Lee had become dependent on Stuart's reliable information about the enemy. In Stuart's absence, Lee had no satisfactory knowledge of the Army of the Potomac and could not act with his usual precision and initiative.

Lee appears to have never fully understood that he had to adjust his leadership style to the new situation. In retrospect, he lamented, "If I [would have] had Stonewall Jackson at Gettysburg, I would have won that fight." Maybe so, but the fact of the matter was that Lee did not have Jackson at Gettysburg, and he should have supervised the subordinates he did have in a way that met their needs and the needs of the situation.

BELOW: After the battle, the Army of Northern Virginia recrossed the Potomac River near Williamsport, much to the chagrin of President Lincoln.

Aftermath

In spite of the Federal victory at Gettysburg, the Civil War would continue for two more long years. Still for many, Gettysburg was the war's most important battle. Its connection to Pickett's Charge, the Lost Cause, and the Gettysburg Address, as well as its solemn gravestones and stately monuments, have secured its hallowed place in the American experience.

Both sides had been badly hurt in the three days of fighting, with Lee suffering 28,063 killed, wounded, and missing and Meade 23,049. The two armies now lay facing each other, nursing their wounds. Meade had won the Battle of Gettysburg, but now the question became what to do with the victory. His men were tired from

FACING PAGE: Cannon face across the battlefield at sunrise. Responsibility for the Gettysburg battlefield was transferred to the National Park Service in 1933.

RIGHT: Major General George Meade turned back the mighty Army of Northern Virginia at Gettysburg.

days of marching and fighting. Dead and wounded soldiers and damaged and discarded equipment filled the battlefield and had to be recovered. Many veteran soldiers, as well as key leaders such as John Reynolds and Winfield Scott Hancock, were killed or wounded.

Meade too was personally exhausted. After the battle, a newspaper reporter found him "stooping and weary," and one of Meade's biographers describes him as "a picture of sorry discomfort." One can only imagine his psychological state. American historian Bruce Catton paints a vivid picture: "Meade was on the road with his troops, an infinitely weary man with dust on his uniform and his gray beard,

feeling responsibility as a paralyzing weight. He had been one of the few men who could have lost the war irretrievably in one day, and he had managed to avoid the mistakes that would have lost it. He would continue to avoid mistakes, even if he had to miss opportunity ... Meade could see all the things that might go wrong ...." Meade was of no mind to exploit his victory, and he seemed content to let Lee withdraw back into Virginia.

Lincoln, however, had other ideas. He announced Meade's success to the nation in restrained tones, withholding from Meade the thanks and praise he had lavished on Ulysses S. Grant after his victory at Vicksburg. Lincoln felt Meade's work was unfinished. It was not time to celebrate yet, and Washington sent Meade instructions that "The opportunity to attack [Lee's] divided forces should not be lost. The President is urgent and anxious that your army should move against [Lee] by forced marches."

In the end, however, Meade mounted only a halfhearted attempt to go after Lee. Some observers comment that Meade appeared to have "escorted" Lee out of the North, rather than pursuing him bent on his destruction. Watching Meade's uninspired effort, Lincoln complained,

LEFT: A statue of Major General Winfield Scott Hancock stands on the battlefield today. He was awarded "the gratitude of the American People, and the Thanks of their Representatives in Congress ... for his gallant, meritorious and conspicuous share in the great and decisive victory."

"I'll be hanged if I could think of anything but an old woman trying to shoo her geese across a creek." Such a tepid pursuit was of no consequence, and Lincoln was beside himself. He wrote Meade, "I do not believe you appreciate the magnitude of the misfortune involved in Lee's escape. He was within your easy grasp, and to have closed upon him would, in connection with our other late successes, have ended the war. As it is, the war will be prolonged indefinitely."

A Lost Opportunity

Many historians share Lincoln's view that after Gettysburg Meade lost an opportunity to end the war. Indeed, it is true that great generals must be audacious. They must take calculated

ABOVE: Pursuit of Lee's army—the scene on the road near Emmitsburg, marching through the rain. Content with his victory, Meade mounted only a token pursuit as Lee's defeated army withdrew back to Virginia.

risks in order to achieve spectacular results. Meade lacked this important characteristic of generalship, and after Gettysburg, he acted as if his mission was accomplished. Edward Stackpole concludes, "Some generals play it safe, forgetting perhaps that war is far from being a safe enterprise. Others take calculated risks when large results are possible. The great Captains have been those who audaciously and aggressively discounted the odds, whether actual or imagined, and by their boldness won important victories… Meade was not [that kind of general]."

Nonetheless, Meade had many defenders on his staff including his engineer Major General Gouverneur Warren and his artilleryman Brigadier General Henry Hunt. To be fair to Meade, any analysis of his actions must be done not from the comfortable view of the detached observer, but from the much more tenuous position that was Meade's perspective. Under such circumstances Meade can be forgiven for

BELOW: The Lutheran Seminary, the county courthouse, and Pennsylvania College's "Old Dorm" were among the many buildings pressed into service as hospitals to care for the wounded.

EXCERPT FROM LETTER OF DWIGHT HENRY CORY DESCRIBING HIS PARTICIPATION IN THE 6TH OHIO VOLUNTEER CAVALRY'S PURSUIT OF LEE'S ARMY

Camp in the Woods near the battlefield of Antiatam [sic], MD
July 12, 1863

Dear Parents, Brothers & Sisters:

I received four letters from home (and its vicinity) day before yesterday. One from Mother, one from Sylvia and one from John and Emily. One from Debra French and one from Libbie Braden. These all were read with great pleasure. What did you do on the 4th to celebrate the birthday of the U.S.? We, the troops of Gen Kilpatrick's brigade, went over the mountain and took 1500 prisoners and 160 wagons loaded with all kinds of stores that they had taken in Pa, and about 100 wounded Rebs. We started in pursuit of the train, about four in the p.m. and rode all night and it rained and was very dark, but this didn't hinder our artillery from sending a shot through five or six wagons as they were going along the road. Then our men, mostly from our reg. charged among them and took the whole thing, including Gen. Jones who was dressed as a citizen. I tell you there is not a general in the whole service that stands higher in the estimation of Old Kill than ours.

Adieu kind friends,
Dwight

playing it safe. He had assumed command under extremely traumatic circumstances and turned back the great Robert E. Lee from Northern soil. That, Meade thought, was enough.

In spite of the incomplete victory, Meade had succeeded in inflicting close to 30,000 casualties on the Army of Northern Virginia, a number amounting to one-third of Lee's total strength. These losses forever blunted Lee's offensive capability, and set the stage for Lieutenant General Ulysses S. Grant to use unrelenting pressure to grind the Army of Northern Virginia into submission.

But until then, Meade had done what none of his predecessors had accomplished. He had truly beaten Lee. Moreover, Meade had stood in the gap at a time when if he had failed, the Union cause would have very likely been lost. Eclipsed in history by Grant's much greater fame, Meade nonetheless did his duty when his country needed him to.

Treating the Casualties

Although the battle was over and the armies gone, Gettysburg, a town of just 2,400 residents, was devastated. Of most immediate concern were the 14,529 Federal and 18,735 Confederate wounded. Lee had been able to evacuate some 12,700 of his wounded when he withdrew across the Potomac, but those left behind relied on the enemy for care. Churches, the Lutheran Seminary, farmhouses and barns, public buildings, and private homes were pressed into service as hospitals, and the small Federal medical staff that remained on the scene was overwhelmed. The situation was exacerbated by then commander of the Army of the Potomac Joseph Hooker's June 19 order that had reduced the Medical Department's transportation to about two wagons per brigade in the march north from Virginia.

Meade's attempt to adjust the order had resulted in confusion, and it was not until July 2 that any of the corps hospital trains began to arrive at Gettysburg, with the exception of those belonging to XII Corps which had traveled with the corps. Into this crisis stepped Doctors Jonathan Letterman and Henry James to direct the efforts of some 1,106 Federal army medical officers reinforced by a large number of medical cadets and local doctors. The seven corps hospitals were set up to augment the makeshift ones and organized treatment got underway. On July 8, authorities began moving the wounded by train to permanent hospitals in Baltimore, York, Harrisburg, and elsewhere. In spite of this herculean effort, by the last week of the month, 1,995 Federals and 2,922 Confederates were too badly injured to travel and remained in desperate need of care.

To meet this need, Camp Letterman was established about a mile (1.6 km) east of Gettysburg in Wolf's Woods along the York Road. This general hospital officially opened on July 22. Between August 5 and 11, all of the Confederate wounded were transported there. The Federal wounded began moving there on August 12, and by August 18, all the corps hospitals outside Gettysburg were broken up. As a result, according to one nurse, Camp Letterman came to house "the very dregs of battle from two armies." To the great credit of the medical personnel who labored there, both Federal and Confederate wounded were treated with no difference in care.

The U.S. Sanitary Commission also provided yeoman's service, furnishing medical supplies, medicine, and equipment. This civilian organization also established a "lodging hospital" in a field along the route of the Western Maryland Railroad that housed soldiers awaiting transportation. Rounding out the heroes were countless ladies of Gettysburg and the surrounding towns that contributed their energies. As a result of these combined efforts, Camp Letterman was able to close on November 20.

With the wounded cared for, the dead remained a problem. Between the two armies, some 7,000 men had been killed, and in some

places unburied bodies lay so thick that they dammed rain-swollen streams into ponds. There was little time or energy for individual graves, and most of the dead were buried in trenches of as many as 200 bodies laid like so many logs of wood. Such burial trenches were especially prevalent at places like Culp's Hill or Little Round Top where the fighting had been

ABOVE: **Some 7,000 Federal and Confederate soldiers were killed at Gettysburg. Many would be buried in mass graves.**

heaviest. Often the graves were so shallow that the work was soon undone by weather or animals. Still other graves were opened by the heart-broken friends and relatives who soon descended on the battlefield in search of their loved ones.

Thousands of dead artillery and cavalry horses and wagon train mules also littered the battlefield. A few were buried, but most were dragged into huge piles and burned. The foul

smoke from these mass cremations polluted the air for miles.

Cemetery Established

When Governor Andrew Curtin visited Gettysburg a few weeks after the battle, he was appalled. Local attorney David Wills was credited with presenting a proposal for the state to purchase land for a cemetery in which the Federal dead could be reinterred. The 17 other states that had soldiers who died in the battle would be invited to contribute to the costs of the reburials and other expenses for the cemetery.

At Curtin's direction, Wills purchased 17 acres (7 ha) on Cemetery Hill, adjacent to the existing Evergreen Cemetery, for $2,475.87. He then commissioned noted landscape architect William Saunders to begin designing what would become the new "Soldiers' National Cemetery." Saunders developed a plan to set the line of graves in concentric arcs curving around a center point which allowed radiating sections to be proportioned in size to accommodate the number of each state's dead while ensuring equal prominence.

On October 15, Wills advertised for bids to remove the dead and rebury them in coffins provided by the Quartermaster Department. F. W. Biesecker submitted the low bid and began removing bodies on October 27. Biesecker's work was less than a third completed on November 19 when some 15,000 people gathered for the dedication of the cemetery. Edward Everett, a highly noted orator and

BELOW: Tombstones in the cemetery at Gettysburg National Military Park. Gettysburg is the final resting place of many who gave "the last full measure."

former Secretary of State and Governor of Massachusetts, was scheduled to be the main speaker. Almost as an afterthought, President Lincoln was invited to provide a "few appropriate remarks" as well. The audience was treated to a 13,607-word, two-hour-long speech by Everett.

Lincoln followed with a speech of two or three minutes and 271 words. At the time, the public response to Everett's remarks was very enthusiastic, and Lincoln's speech was barely noticed. Ultimately, however, the simple eloquence of the "Gettysburg Address" would enshrine it as one of America's most memorable pieces of prose. Everett recognized its brilliance, reportedly writing to Lincoln that "I should be glad, if I could flatter myself that I came as near to the central idea of the occasion, in two hours, as you did in two minutes."

Gettysburg National Military Park

The next major step in the preservation of the battlefield occurred in 1864 when a group of concerned citizens established the Gettysburg Battlefield Memorial Association (GBMA). Armed with $6,000 appropriated by the state of Pennsylvania, the GBMA purchased key tracts of land on Culp's Hill, Cemetery Hill, and Little Round Top. This initial surge, however, lost

LEFT: Troops march through Gettysburg on the day of the dedication. On November 19, 1863, President Lincoln spoke a little over two minutes at the dedication of the Gettysburg National Cemetery.

RIGHT: This Matthew Brady photograph hangs in Hanover Junction, where President Lincoln's official train arrived en route to Gettysburg for the dedication of the Soldiers' National Cemetery. The man in front of the center window, wearing a top hat, is believed to be President Lincoln.

momentum, only to be revived in 1878 when the Pennsylvania Grand Army of the Republic met at Gettysburg.

This encampment marked the beginning of the emplacement of monuments on the battlefield. The first was located at the place on Little Round Top where Colonel Strong Vincent was shot. The next year, survivors of the 2nd Massachusetts Infantry attached a tablet to a boulder near Spangler's Spring to commemorate their role in the battle. In 1880, the 91st Pennsylvania placed a monument on Little Round Top. Others followed and in 1883 Massachusetts established the precedent of states honoring their soldiers by appropriating $500 for each of its units for monuments. Other states followed Massachusetts's lead. New York and Pennsylvania were particularly generous, allocating $1,500 for each of their units.

By 1894, the GBMA owned 600 acres (240 ha) of land which contained over 300 monuments and 17 miles (27 km) of roads. It was a massive responsibility and in 1895, the GBMA willingly transferred its holdings to the War Department. Gettysburg veteran Major General and Congressman Daniel Sickles was instrumental in the process.

The War Department administered its responsibilities through a Federally-appointed commission comprised of three Civil War veterans, one of which was a Confederate. This commission oversaw the development of the new "Gettysburg National Park" as a memorial to both armies by identifying and marking the lines of battle. The venerable Colonel John Nicholson chaired the commission until his death in 1922. He was succeeded by Colonel E. B. Cope who had previously been the park's engineer. Under such capable leadership, the War Department produced significant improvements. The road network was expanded to over 30 miles (50 km). Tablets were added to describe the dispositions of brigades, divisions, and corps. Civil War cannons were acquired and placed to mark the location of batteries during the battle. A particularly important development occurred in 1915 when the commission licensed 91 trained battlefield guides.

Administration of the park was transferred to the National Park Service, a bureau of the Department of the Interior, in 1933. During the Great Depression, members of the Civilian Conservation Corps helped maintain the grounds, but there was little money available for development. New life was breathed into the park in 1956 when Congress endorsed "Mission 66" to develop all parks. Among

ABOVE: This draft of the Gettysburg Address is called the "Nicolay Copy" because it was once owned by John George Nicolay, Lincoln's private secretary. The first page of this copy is on White House (then Executive Mansion) stationery.

LEFT: Lincoln's Gettysburg Address is one of the most famous pieces of American oratory. This is the only confirmed photo of Abraham Lincoln at Gettysburg, taken some three hours before the speech.

THE GETTYSBURG ADDRESS

Four score and seven years ago our fathers brought forth on this continent a new nation, conceived in liberty, and dedicated to the proposition that all men are created equal.

Now we are engaged in a great civil war, testing whether that nation, or any nation, so conceived and so dedicated, can long endure. We are met on a great battlefield of that war. We have come to dedicate a portion of that field, as a final resting place for those who here gave their lives that that nation might live. It is altogether fitting and proper that we should do this.

But, in a larger sense, we cannot dedicate, we cannot consecrate, we cannot hallow this ground. The brave men, living and dead, who struggled here, have consecrated it, far above our poor power to add or detract. The world will little note, nor long remember what we say here, but it can never forget what they did here. It is for us the living, rather, to be dedicated here to the unfinished work which they who fought here have thus far so nobly advanced. It is rather for us to be here dedicated to the great task remaining before us—that from these honored dead we take increased devotion to that cause for which they gave the last full measure of devotion—that we here highly resolve that these dead shall not have died in vain—that this nation, under God, shall have a new birth of freedom—and that government of the people, by the people, for the people, shall not perish from the earth.

U.S. President Abraham Lincoln

the improvements this program meant for Gettysburg was the construction of a Visitor Center in 1962. Included in the many impressive exhibits at the center is a Cyclorama that dramatically depicts Pickett's Charge.

Less well-received was the Gettysburg National Tower, a 307-foot (94 m) observation tower built by private interests outside the park's boundaries in 1974. Although the tower attracted many visitors, it was roundly decried as an eyesore and an inappropriate commercialization of hallowed ground. It was demolished in 2000 to the great satisfaction of preservationists.

Today Gettysburg, like many Civil War battlefields, struggles to balance heritage and progress. In 2003, a five-year plan to restore the Cyclorama was initiated. A new $103 million Museum and Visitor Center was opened in 2008. In 2009, the David Wills House opened in downtown Gettysburg to showcase the story of Lincoln, the Gettysburg Address, and the aftermath of the battle. A controversial measure to bring a casino to a hotel about 2 miles (3.2 km) from the park's gate would have provided an economic boost to the town but was defeated in 2011 thanks to the efforts of historians and preservationists. Still, the sanctity of the battlefield competes with ghost tours for the attention of the

RIGHT: The Pennsylvania Monument is one of approximately 1,328 monuments, markers, and memorials at Gettysburg National Military Park.

over one million visitors that come to the park each year. Nonetheless, with its museum housing 300,000 objects and artifacts and 700,000 archival materials, and its 6,000 acres (2,400 ha) boasting 1,328 monuments, memorials, and markers, Gettysburg National Military Park has succeeded in its mission to honor the more than 165,000 brave soldiers in blue and gray who fought this pivotal battle of the Civil War.

The Lost Cause

In addition to efforts to preserve the battlefield itself, Gettysburg also played an important role in how the wider Civil War would be remembered in the national consciousness. Faced with the loss of the war and the socio-economic changes that accompanied it, the South struggled to make sense of its defeat. The "Lost Cause" explanation, in which the Confederacy was portrayed in a decidedly heroic and virtuous way, soon gained ascendancy. Edward Pollard, a Richmond newspaper editor, is given credit for coining the phrase in a book he wrote in 1866.

The Lost Cause ideology minimizes the role of slavery as a cause of the Civil War. Instead, secession was motivated by the South's desire to preserve the political notion of state's rights. This interpretation made the Confederate cause a noble one, committed to principle rather than material interests. The Lost Cause also depicted the South as a Christian society, especially in contrast with the economically motivated and industrialized North. The Christian examples

of General Robert E. Lee, Lieutenant General Stonewall Jackson, and others fueled this assertion, as did the piety, virtue, and sacrifice of Southern women.

Perhaps most tellingly, the Lost Cause explained the Confederate defeat as the result of overwhelming Federal resources. The Confederate cause was noble and its people and way of life superior, but it could not stand against the manpower, money, and industry of the North. In this way, Southern pride was

ABOVE: Visitors view the Gettysburg Cyclorama, a 360-degree oil on canvas painting 359 feet long by 27 feet high (109 x 8 m), which depicts Pickett's Charge.

RIGHT: Entitled "The Lost Cause" by North Carolina author P. C. Carlton, this 1872 lithograph includes actual Confederate currency arranged in an octagonal design. A central illustration of a Confederate flag against a starry sky is set within a shield, which in turn is surrounded by five oval portraits of Southern leader Jefferson Davis and generals Robert E. Lee, Stonewall Jackson, Joseph E. Johnston, and Pierre Gustave Toutant de Beauregard.

preserved and responsibility for defeat was transferred. Pickett's Charge became the classic battlefield representation of the Lost Cause.

Excerpt from William Faulkner's Intruder in the Dust

For every Southern boy, fourteen years old, not once but whenever he wants it there is an instant when it's still not yet two o'clock on that July afternoon in 1863, the brigades are in position behind the rail fence, the guns are laid and ready in the woods and the furled flags are already loosened to break out and Pickett himself with his long oiled ringlets and his hat in one hand probably and his sword in the other looking up the hill waiting for Longstreet to give the word and it's all in the balance, it hasn't happened yet, it hasn't even begun yet, it not only hasn't begun yet but there is still time for it not to begin against that position and those circumstances, which made more men than Garnett and Kemper and Armistead and Wilcox look grave yet it's going to begin, we all know that, we have come too far with too much at stake and that moment doesn't need even a fourteen-year-old boy to think *This time, Maybe this time* with all this much to lose and all this much to gain.

Today Gettysburg stands as a multifaceted reminder of this pivotal event in the history of the United States. It represents different things to different people. To some it is the climactic victory that saved the Union. To others it is a poignant manifestation of the Lost Cause. To some it is the horrific loss of several thousand Americans lives. To others it is the glory of Pickett's Charge. To some it is the hallowed ground of the Soldiers' National Cemetery. To others it is the crass commercialism of the tourist trade. But whatever form the memory takes, as then Vice President Lyndon Johnson said on Memorial Day 1963, "We, the living, have not forgotten—and the world will never forget—the deeds or the words of Gettysburg."

BELOW: **This group of Confederate veterans commemorates the 50th anniversary of the battle in 1913.**

Key Federal Leaders

The Federal command at Gettysburg was an eclectic group. It included newspapermen like Francis Barlow, foreigners like Carl Schurz, and professors like Joshua Chamberlain. Some were political generals like Daniel Sickles and others were military professionals like John Sedgwick.

There were young men like George Custer and much older men like James Wadsworth. Some were veterans of the Mexican War like George Sykes, others were fresh out of West Point like Alonzo Cushing, and there were native Pennsylvanians like John Reynolds. Courageous men like Alexander Webb would win the Medal of Honor for their bravery while Alexander

Schimmelfennig spent most of the battle hiding behind a wood pile. If there was a common theme, it was perhaps that many were new to their job. Not the least among these was George Meade, who had assumed command of the Army of the Potomac only days before the battle. Under the circumstances, Meade and his men faced a complicated and perilous task. Failure could well be disastrous to the Union. They would have to rise to meet this momentous occasion. The very fate of the nation depended on them.

FACING PAGE: Major General George Meade and his staff are shown here in front of Wallack's House in Culpeper, Virginia after the Battle of Gettysburg. Unsure of Lee's location or even the locations of all elements of the Army of the Potomac, Meade certainly was not so relaxed when he assumed command on June 28.

RIGHT: An able commander-in-chief, President Abraham Lincoln had difficulty finding generals that shared his strategic vision of destroying Lee's Army.

Ames, Adelbert

(1835–1933)
Rank: Brigadier General
Unit: 2nd Brigade, 1st Division, XI Corps

Adelbert Ames graduated from the United States Military Academy at West Point in 1861 and was awarded the Medal of Honor for his performance at First Manassas. After recovering from his wounds, he commanded during the Peninsula Campaign, at Antietam, and at Fredericksburg. He served as Major General George Meade's aide at Chancellorsville before being promoted to brigadier general on May 20, 1863. He led a brigade in the XI Corps at the beginning of Gettysburg and a division on the second and third days of the battle.

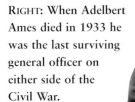

RIGHT: When Adelbert Ames died in 1933 he was the last surviving general officer on either side of the Civil War.

Barlow, Francis

(1834–1896)
Rank: Brigadier General
Unit: 1st Division, XI Corps

Francis Barlow worked as a lawyer for the *New-York Tribune* before the war. After service during the Peninsula Campaign and at Antietam, he was promoted to brigadier general on September 19, 1862. He commanded a brigade at Chancellorsville and was severely wounded while leading a division at Gettysburg during the first day's fighting. He was left for dead and captured by Confederate Brigadier General John Gordon who attended to the wounded Federal officer's injuries. Gordon enjoyed telling a much embellished version of the encounter after the war.

Birney, David

(1825–1864)
Rank: Major General
Unit: 1st Division, III Corps

David Birney was the son of the abolitionist James Birney. He recruited a regiment largely at his own expense and was made a

RIGHT: A businessman and lawyer pre-war, David Birney was one of the Federal Army's political generals.

brigadier general on February 17, 1862. He was court-martialed and acquitted of disobedience to an order at the Battle of Seven Pines. He served well at Chancellorsville and was promoted to major general on May 20, 1863. At Gettysburg he assumed command of the III Corps when Major General Daniel Sickles was wounded.

Buford, John

(1826–1863)
Rank: Brigadier General
Unit: 1st Division, Cavalry Corps

John Buford graduated from West Point in 1848 and served in the West before the Civil War. He demonstrated excellent skill as a cavalryman at First and Second Manassas and was promoted to brigadier general on June 1, 1863. Riding ahead of the army in Pennsylvania, he spotted the enemy northwest of Gettysburg, and, recognizing the importance of the situation, prepared to hold McPherson's Ridge. This critical action allowed time for elements of the I Corps to arrive and reinforce the position.

Chamberlain, Joshua

(1828–1914)
Rank: Colonel
Unit: 20th Maine Rgt, 3rd Bde, 1st Div, V Corps

Joshua Chamberlain was a professor at Bowdoin College before the Civil War. He

ABOVE: Seeing the approaching Confederate army on July 1, John Buford famously announced, "The devil's to pay."

served at Antietam, Fredericksburg, and Chancellorsville, and was promoted to colonel on May 20, 1863. As commander of the 20th Maine at Gettysburg, he was instrumental in holding Little Round Top, the key to the outcome of the second day's fighting. He was awarded the Medal of Honor for his actions

there. His story is told in Michael Shaara's historical novel, *The Killer Angels.*

Medal of Honor Citation for Joshua Chamberlain

The President of the United States of America, in the name of Congress, takes pleasure in presenting the Medal of Honor to Colonel Joshua Lawrence Chamberlain, United States Army, for extraordinary heroism on 2 July 1863, while serving with 20th Maine Infantry, in action at Gettysburg, Pennsylvania, for daring heroism and great tenacity in holding his position on the Little Round Top against repeated assaults, and carrying the advance position on the Great Round Top.

Curtin, Andrew

(1817–1894)
Politician

Andrew Curtin was the governor of Pennsylvania from 1861 to 1867. His election as a Republican provided an important boost to Abraham Lincoln's first presidential campaign. During the Civil War, Curtin and Lincoln enjoyed a close relationship, and Curtin visited the White House several times. He was instrumental in organizing Pennsylvania's mobilization for war, and in September 1862, he convened the Loyal War Governors' Conference at Altoona which brought together 13 governors of Union states to discuss the war effort, state

Harrisburg, PA
June 16, 1863

For nearly a week past it has been publicly known that the rebels, in force, were about to enter Pennsylvania.

On the 12th instant, an urgent call was made on the people to raise a Departmental Army Corps for the defense of the State. Yesterday, under the proclamation of the President, the militia was called out. To-day a new and pressing exhortation has been given to furnish men.

Philadelphia has not responded. Meanwhile the enemy is 6 miles this side of Chambersburg, and advancing rapidly. Our capital is threatened, and we may be disgraced by its fall, while the men who should be driving these outlaws from our soil are quarreling about the possible term of service

for six months. It never was intended to keep them beyond the continuance of the emergency. You all know this by what happened when the militia was called out last autumn. You then trusted your Government, and were not deceived. Trust it again now. I will accept men without reference to the six months. If you do not wish to bear the ignomity of shrinking from the defense of your State, come forward at once, close your places of business, and apply your heads to the work. Come in such organizations as you can form. Gen. Couch has appointed Lieut.-Col. Ruff to superintend your organization. Report to him immediately.

A. G. CURTIN
Governor of Pennsylvania, 1861–1867

troop quotas, and support for Lincoln and the Emancipation Proclamation.

During the Gettysburg Campaign, Curtin was active in alerting the nation to the threat posed by Lee's move north. After the battle, Curtin was a driving force behind the creation of the Soldiers' National Cemetery (also known as the Gettysburg National Cemetery).

LEFT: As Governor of Pennsylvania, Andrew Curtin was active before, during, and after the Battle of Gettysburg.

Cushing, Alonzo

(1841–1863)
Rank: 1st Lieutenant
Unit: Battery A, 4th U.S. Artillery

Alonzo Cushing graduated from West Point in 1861 and fought at First Manassas, as well as the Peninsula Campaign, at Antietam, and at Fredericksburg. As a first lieutenant at Gettysburg, he commanded Battery A, 4th U.S.

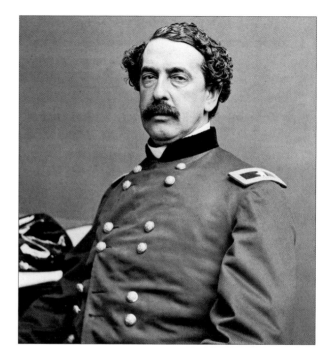

LEFT: Most famous for his "Last Stand" at the Battle of Little Bighorn, George Custer began his career during the Civil War.

RIGHT: Abner Doubleday is often incorrectly given credit for inventing the game of baseball.

Artillery. Although he was severely wounded, he and his men manned their guns and helped repulse Pickett's Charge at the "High Watermark of the Confederacy." He is immortalized in Stephen Vincent Benét's poem, *John Brown's Body*, as "Cushing ran down the last of his guns to the battle-line. The rest had been smashed to scrap by Lee's artillery fire. He held his guts in his hand as the charge came up the wall. And his gun spoke out for him once before he fell to the ground."

Custer, George

(1839–1876)

Rank: Brigadier General
Unit: 2nd Brigade, 3rd Division, Cavalry Corps

George Custer graduated last in his class from West Point in 1861. He quickly showed an aptitude as a cavalryman he had not demonstrated as a cadet and was promoted from first lieutenant to brigadier

general on June 29, 1863 at the age of 23. A few days later he was commanding a cavalry brigade at Gettysburg.

Doubleday, Abner

(1819–1893)

Rank: Major General
Unit: 3rd Division, I Corps

Abner Doubleday graduated from West Point in 1842 and was among the besieged Federal soldiers at Fort Sumter. After serving at the battles of Second Manassas, Antietam, and Fredericksburg, he was promoted to major general on November 29, 1862 and commanded a division at Chancellorsville. At Gettysburg, he assumed command of I Corps after Major General John Reynolds was killed. Doubleday was known for his slow, deliberate manner, and Major Generals Oliver Howard and Winfield Scott Hancock accused him, perhaps unfairly, of mishandling the corps on July 1. Based on this report, Major General George Meade placed Major General John Newton in command of I Corps. Doubleday considered Howard's report an "unfounded accusation" and remained resentful of Howard and Meade for this slight to his reputation.

EXCERPT FROM GIBBON'S OFFICIAL REPORT OF HIS DIVISION'S ACTIONS ON JULY 3— BALTIMORE, MD, August 7, 1863

Maj. W. G. MITCHELL,
Acting Assistant Adjutant-General, Second Corps

SIR: Skirmishing continued all along the line at intervals during the morning, and some little artillery firing occurred, but at 1 o'clock (at which time, General Hancock having resumed command of the corps, I returned to my division) the enemy opened with his artillery all along his line, and for two hours the most terrific shower of shot and shell continued, ably responded to by our batteries. At the end of that time the fire on both sides slackened, and the enemy displayed his first line coming out of the woods, stud preceded by a heavy line of skirmishers, which commenced immediately to push ours back. The line moved steadily to the front in a way to excite the admiration of every one, and was followed by a second and third, extending all along our front as far as the eye could reach. Our guns were run well forward, so as to give them a good sweep over the ground, loaded with canister, and the men warned to keep well under cover, and to reserve their fire until the enemy got well within range. As the front line came up, it was met with such a withering fire of canister and musketry as soon melted it away, but still on they came from behind, pressing forward to the wall. By this time most of our artillerymen had fallen, and but an occasional cannon shot along our part of the line interrupted the continuous rattle of musketry. The right of the enemy's line did not extend as far as the left of my division, and, while urging forward some of my left regiments to take his line in flank, I was wounded and left the field. The rest is told by the brigade reports.

I am, sir, very respectfully, your obedient servant,

JOHN GIBBON
Brigadier-General of Volunteers,
Commanding Division

Gibbon, John
(1827–1896)
Rank: Brigadier General
Unit: 2nd Division, II Corps

John Gibbon graduated from West Point in 1847 and fought in the Seminole Wars. He was made brigadier general on May 2, 1862 and commanded at Second Manassas, Antietam, and Fredericksburg where he was seriously wounded. He commanded the 2nd Division of II Corps, and on two occasions held temporary command of the corps. Major General George Meade correctly predicted to Gibbon on July 2 that "If Lee attacks tomorrow, it will be on your front." Gibbon's division was in fact in the thick of Pickett's Charge, and he was wounded during that fighting. The tablet at his monument at Gettysburg reads, "He has a keen eye and is as bold as a lion."

Hancock, Winfield Scott

(1824–1886)
Rank: Major General
Unit: II Corps

Winfield Scott Hancock graduated from West Point in 1844 and fought in the Second Seminole War and the Mexican-American War. He was a quartermaster officer in California at the beginning of the Civil War and his farewell there to Lewis Armistead and other old army friends bound for the Confederacy is the subject of many romantic portrayals. He was promoted to brigadier general on September 23, 1861 and commanded a brigade during the Peninsula Campaign where he was highly praised for his actions, especially at Williamsburg. Major General George McClellan felt that "Hancock

was superb" and he is often referred to as "Hancock the Superb."

Hancock fought at Antietam, Fredericksburg, and Chancellorsville and was promoted to major general on November 29, 1862. He commanded the II Corps at Gettysburg. He assumed control, over the objections of Major General Oliver Howard, of the field during the confusion of the first day and helped restore order to the shaken Federal forces. He was severely wounded defending against Pickett's Charge. On April 21, 1866 he received the Thanks of Congress for his actions at Gettysburg.

Hooker, Joseph

(1814–1879)
Rank: Major General
Unit: Army of the Potomac

Joseph Hooker graduated from West Point in 1837 and fought in the Second Seminole War and during the Mexican-American War. On May 17, 1861, he was appointed a brigadier general and assigned to the Washington defenses. He commanded a division during the Peninsula Campaign and prematurely initiated action at Williamsburg. A series of Associated Press releases during the Seven Days Campaign were

FACING PAGE: Before he was relieved of command, Joseph Hooker was able to implement several administrative reforms in the Army of the Potomac such as improving the intelligence service.

HOOKER'S FAREWELL ADDRESS TO THE ARMY HEADQUARTERS, ARMY OF THE POTOMAC

FREDERICK, MD,
June 28, 1863

In conformity with the orders of the War Department, dated June 27, 1863, I relinquish the command of the Army of the Potomac. It is transferred to Major General George G. Meade, a brave and accomplished officer, who has nobly earned the confidence and esteem of the army on many a well fought field. Impressed with the belief that my usefulness as the commander of the Army of the Potomac is impaired, I part from it, yet not without the deepest emotion. The sorrow of parting with the comrades of so many battles is relieved by the conviction that the courage and devotion of this army will never cease nor fail; that it will yield to my successor, as it has to me a willing and hearty support. With the earnest prayer that the triumph of its arms may bring successes worthy of it and the nation, I bid it farewell.

JOSEPH HOOKER
Major General

headed "Fighting Joe Hooker," and newspapers all over the country simply removed the hyphen and used "Fighting Joe Hooker" instead. The nickname stuck.

Hooker was promoted to major general on

May 5, 1862 and commanded a corps at Antietam and the two-corps Center Grand Division at Fredericksburg. After that battle, he accelerated his disloyal and ambitious attacks against Major General Ambrose Burnside and was named commander of the Army of the Potomac on January 26, 1863. He was soundly defeated at Chancellorsville and, much to the displeasure of President Abraham Lincoln, was slow and ineffective as General Robert E. Lee began to move north. Lincoln relieved him of his command on June 28 and replaced him with Major General George Meade on the eve of the Battle of Gettysburg. The *New-York Tribune* reported, "The relieving of Hooker is received with a kind of apathetic indifference by the army, although many are loud in denouncing the act at this particular time." In spite of his loss of command, Hooker received the Thanks of Congress for what he had done to defend Baltimore and Washington, D.C. against Lee's advance north. Meade, who also was so honored for Gettysburg, was incredulous that Hooker received such recognition.

Howard, Oliver Otis

(1830–1909)
Rank: Major General
Unit: XI Corps

Oliver Otis Howard graduated from West Point in 1854. After fighting at First Manassas, he was made brigadier general on September 3, 1861

seniority, took charge. Howard's performance that day was mixed and indecisive although he was given, perhaps overly generously, the Thanks of Congress for his part in establishing a defensive line around Cemetery Hill. He is better remembered for his work with the Freedman's Bureau after the war.

LEFT: Oliver Otis Howard's religious piety led him to be known as "the Christian General."

BELOW: Although brave in combat, Andrew Humphreys (seated) had a reputation for personal vanity that made him unpopular with many of his men.

Humphreys, Andrew

(1810–1883)
Rank: Brigadier General
Unit: 2nd Division, III Corps

Andrew Humphreys graduated from West Point in 1831. He fought in the Seminole Wars and worked as a civil engineer before the Civil War.

and commanded a brigade during the Peninsula Campaign where he was seriously wounded and lost his right arm. He was back in action after just 80 days. Howard commanded a division at Antietam and Fredericksburg. He was promoted to major general on November 29, 1862. At Chancellorsville, his XI Corps was surprised and routed by Lieutenant General Stonewall Jackson's flank attack.

During the Battle of Gettysburg, he commanded the field on July 1 after the death of Major General John Reynolds until Major General Winfield Scott Hancock arrived and, after some argument with Howard over

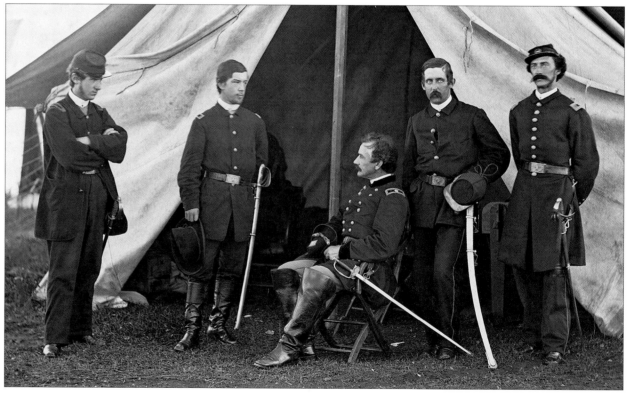

He was promoted to brigadier general on April 28, 1862 and served as Chief Topographical Engineer of the Army of the Potomac during the Peninsula Campaign. He commanded a division at Antietam, Fredericksburg, and Chancellorsville. At Gettysburg, he commanded the 2nd Division of III Corps and fought well, resisting the Confederate attacks made possible by the salient created by Major General Daniel Sickles on the second day of the battle. On the strength of his performance at Gettysburg, Humphreys was promoted to major general on July 8, 1863 and became Major General George Meade's Chief of Staff.

Hunt, Henry

(1819–1889)
Rank: Brigadier General
Unit: Chief of Artillery, Army of the Potomac

Henry Hunt graduated from West Point in 1839 and trained in artillery while serving under Lieutenant James Duncan in Mexico. In what Brigadier General William Worth would call a "brilliant exhibition of courage and conduct," Hunt especially distinguished himself at Chapultepec, pushing his gun up to a Mexican artillery position, and, firing "muzzle to muzzle," reduced the resistance. He served at First Manassas, during the Peninsula Campaign, and at Antietam, and was promoted to brigadier general on September 15, 1862.

As the Chief of Artillery for the Army of the Potomac, Hunt initiated a reorganization of the artillery and centralized its command, grouping batteries into brigades

Henry Hunt's artillery was critical to the success of the Army of the Potomac at Gettysburg.

and placing them under the leadership of a corps chief of artillery. Additionally, the Artillery Reserve, a body of 100 guns including the horse and siege cannon, was reorganized into five artillery brigades. The Reserve could be dispatched partially or collectively to reinforce batteries. This ability to mass its artillery assets gave the Federal army an advantage at Gettysburg. Most notably, on July 3, Hunt was able to position 77 guns along a narrow front on the left-center of the Federal line to help defeat Pickett's Charge.

Lincoln, Abraham

(1809–1865)
President of the United States

Although having only minimal military experience as a militia captain in the Black Hawk War, President Abraham Lincoln proved to be a highly capable commander in chief. He struggled to find a suitable commander of the Army of the Potomac, and when he appointed Major General George Meade to that position on June 28, 1863, he became the sixth officer Lincoln had tried in the east.

One of Lincoln's problems with his commanders was his inability to convince them to share his assessment that General Robert E. Lee's army was their objective. As Lee moved north, Lincoln pressed Major General Joseph Hooker: "If the head of the animal is at the fords of the Potomac and the tail at Culpeper

Court House, it must be very thin somewhere. Why don't you strike it?" Even after the victory at Gettysburg, Lincoln complained to Meade, "I do not believe you appreciate the magnitude of the misfortune involved in Lee's escape."

Lincoln has a special connection with Gettysburg as a result of his eloquent "Gettysburg Address," delivered at the dedication of the Soldiers' National Cemetery there on November 19, 1863.

Many an American elementary school student can recite at least "Four score and seven years ago..." from Abraham Lincoln's Gettysburg Address.

EXCERPT FROM PRESIDENT DWIGHT EISENHOWER'S SPEECH MARKING THE CENTENNIAL OF LINCOLN'S GETTYSBURG ADDRESS, November 19, 1963

We mark today the centennial of an immortal address. We stand where Abraham Lincoln stood as, a century ago, he gave to the world words as moving in their solemn cadence as they are timeless in their meaning. Little wonder it is that, as here we sense his deep dedication to freedom, our own dedication takes added strength.

Lincoln had faith that the ancient drums of Gettysburg, throbbing mutual defiance from the battle lines of the blue and the gray, would one day beat in unison, to summon a people, happily united in peace, to fulfill, generation by generation, a noble destiny. His faith has been justified—but the unfinished work of which he spoke in 1863 is still unfinished; because of human frailty, it always will be.

Where we see the serenity with which time has invested this hallowed ground, Lincoln saw the scarred earth and felt the press of personal grief.

Yet he lifted his eyes to the future, the future that is our present. He foresaw a new birth of freedom, a freedom and equality for all which, under God, would restore the purpose and meaning of America, defining a goal that challenges each of us to attain his full stature of citizenship.

We read Lincoln's sentiments, we ponder his words—the beauty of the sentiments he expressed enthralls us; the majesty of his words holds us spellbound—but we have not paid to his message its just tribute until we—ourselves—live it. For well he knew that to live for country is a duty, as demanding as is the readiness to die for it. So long as this truth remains our guiding light, self-government in this nation will never die.

PRESIDENT DWIGHT D. EISENHOWER

Meade, George

(1815–1872)

Rank: Major General

Unit: Army of the Potomac

George Meade graduated from West Point in 1835 and served in the Mexican-American War. A Pennsylvanian, Meade was made a brigadier general on August 31, 1861 with the advocacy of Pennsylvania Governor Andrew Curtin. Although Meade had little previous experience leading troops, he was given command of one of the three Pennsylvania brigades. He commanded a brigade during the Peninsula Campaign and at Second Manassas and a division at Antietam and Fredericksburg. He was promoted to major general on November 29, 1862 and led the V Corps at Chancellorsville.

Meade was known to have an irascible personality and short temper. He was also conscientious, dutiful, and courageous, and had little ambition for high command. Upon receiving word he would assume command of the Army of the Potomac on June 28, 1863, he protested "Why me? Why not Reynolds?" Indeed, many thought that Major General John Reynolds would have been a more qualified

LEFT: George Meade, the "Old Snapping Turtle," saved the day for the Federal cause at Gettysburg.

choice. Some sources believe Reynolds had been offered the position after Chancellorsville but declined the offer because he thought Washington would not give him a free hand in exercising the command. Other theorists believe Meade was preferred because his birth in Spain prevented him from having any presidential aspirations. For whatever the reason, President Abraham Lincoln picked Meade who overcame his initial reluctance to save the Union with his victory at Gettysburg. Although Meade won the Thanks of Congress for his service, Lincoln was

EXCERPT FROM MEADE'S OFFICIAL REPORT OF THE BATTLE OF GETTYSBURG— HEADQUARTERS ARMY OF THE POTOMAC, October 1, 1863

Major-General, Commanding.
Brig. Gen. LORENZO THOMAS,
Adjutant-General, U.S. Army, Washington, D.C.

GENERAL:
The result of the campaign may be briefly stated in the defeat of the enemy at Gettysburg, his compulsory evacuation of Pennsylvania and Maryland, and withdrawal from the upper valley of the Shenandoah, and in the capture of 3 guns, 41 standards, and 13,621 prisoners; 24,978 small-arms were collected on the battle-field. Our own losses were very severe, amounting, as will be seen by the accompanying return, to 2,834 killed, 13,709 wounded, and 6,643 missing; in all, 23,186.

It is impossible in a report of this nature to enumerate all the instances of gallantry and good conduct which distinguished such a hard-fought field as Gettysburg. The reports of corps commands and their subordinates, herewith submitted, will furnish all information upon this subject. I will only add my tribute to the heroic bravery of the whole army, officers and men, which, under the blessing of Divine Providence, enabled a crowning victory to be obtained, which I feel confident the country will never cease to bear in grateful remembrance.

Very respectfully, your obedient servant,
GEO. G. MEADE,
Commanding

frustrated that Meade did not aggressively pursue General Robert E. Lee's army after the battle. Seeking a more aggressive commander, Lincoln promoted Ulysses S. Grant to lieutenant general and brought him east to serve as general-in-chief. Although Grant chose to make his headquarters with the Army of the Potomac in the field, Meade remained its operational commander.

Pleasonton, Alfred

(1824–1897)
Rank: Major General
Unit: Cavalry Corps

Alfred Pleasonton graduated from West Point in 1844 and served on the frontier, in the Mexican-American War, and the Seminole Wars. Early in the Civil War, he helped defend Washington, D.C., and then fought during the Peninsula Campaign. He was promoted to brigadier general on July 18, 1862. Pleasonton commanded a cavalry division at Antietam, Fredericksburg, and Chancellorsville. He replaced Major General George Stoneman as commander of the Cavalry Corps on June 7 and was promoted to major general on June 22, 1863. He clashed with Major General Jeb Stuart during the Battle at Brandy Station on June 9. In so doing, Pleasonton confirmed General Robert E. Lee's movements north from Fredericksburg. In holding its own against Stuart, the Federal cavalry gained a new

confidence. Nonetheless, Pleasonton turned in an uninspired performance for the remainder of the Gettysburg Campaign.

Reynolds, John

(1820–1863)
Rank: Major General
Unit: I Corps

John Reynolds graduated from West Point in 1841 and served in the Mexican-American War and in the West. When the Civil War began, he

FACING PAGE: Accounts differ over how Reynolds was killed, but the prevailing theory attributes it to a Confederate sharpshooter.

LEFT: Alfred Pleasonton was quick to exaggerate the extent of his success at Brandy Station.

BELOW: At the time of his death at Gettysburg, many considered John Reynolds to be the best general in the Federal Army.

LETTER FROM PENNSYLVANIA GOVERNOR ANDREW CURTIN TO REYNOLDS'S BROTHER JAMES, July 3, 1863

JAMES L. REYNOLDS, ESQ.
Lancaster, PA

Sir:
I have hoped until now to be at the funeral of your brother, Major General John F. Reynolds, and to testify by my presence something of the high esteem in which I held him as a gentleman and a soldier while he lived, and the profound sorrow I feel at his death.

I know however that he would not have wished me in this hour of peril to neglect the safety of the state he loved so well, and in whose defense he so willingly died, even to do honor to his memory.

As a General, the whole nation honored and mourns him, but Pennsylvania has reason to cherish with especial pride, alike the noble qualities of character which led him to his high command, and his chivalric courage on the historic battle-field where he closed his life so gloriously.

Very respectfully,
Your obt. sert.
A.G. CURTIN

was the Commandant of Cadets at West Point. He was made brigadier general on August 20, 1861 and led a brigade during the Peninsula Campaign. He commanded a division at Second Manassas and I Corps at Fredericksburg. He was promoted to major general on November 29, 1862. He was highly respected in the army and reportedly was offered and declined command of the Army of the Potomac after the Battle of Chancellorsville. Reynolds was killed—probably by a sharpshooter—during the first day's fighting at Gettysburg while trying to rush reinforcements to the aid of Brigadier General John Buford's cavalry.

Schimmelfennig, Alexander

(1824–1865)
Rank: Brigadier General
Unit: 1st Brigade, 3rd Division, XI Corps

Alexander Schimmelfennig was a Prussian officer who fled to the United States after the revolution of 1848. He was promoted to brigadier general on November 29, 1862 and commanded a division in XI Corps at Gettysburg. His unit was overrun on the first day's fighting. Schimmelfennig eluded capture and fled into the town of Gettysburg where he was knocked off his horse by a stray bullet. He found refugee from the pursuing Confederate soldiers in the home of Henry and Catherine Garlach where he remained in hiding for the next three days.

Gettysburg Marker "A Union General Escapes Capture"

Today in Gettysburg at the intersection of Court Alley and Breckenridge Street a marker commemorates Schimmelfennig's adventure. It reads: "In 1863, this building to your right, was the home and cabinetmaker's shop of Henry Garlach and family. Cut off during the Union retreat to Cemetery Hill, General Alexander Schimmelfennig was able to avoid capture by the Confederates, when he hid here for three days in the back yard, shielded behind a stack of firewood and a hog slop barrel situated along the front of the kitchen woodshed. General Schimmelfennig was sustained with food and water secretly delivered to him by Mrs. Catherine Garlach, when she went to feed the family hogs."

Schurz, Carl

(1829–1906)
Rank: Major General
Unit: 3rd Division, XI Corps

Carl Schurz was one of the highly educated "Latin Farmers" that came to the United States from Germany after the revolution of 1848. He was appointed brigadier general on April 15,

1862 based on his abolitionist and political credentials rather than on any military experience. He commanded a division at Second Manassas and at Chancellorsville. He

RIGHT: "Uncle John" Sedgwick was popular with his soldiers. He survived Gettysburg only to be killed the next year in fighting near Spotsylvania Courthouse.

was made major general on March 17, 1863. He temporarily assumed command of the XI Corps during the tumult of the first day at Gettysburg.

Sedgwick, John

(1813–1864)
Rank: Major General
 Unit: VI Corps

John Sedgwick graduated from West Point in 1837. He fought in the Seminole Wars, the Mexican-American War, and in the West. He was appointed brigadier general on August 31, 1861 and commanded a division during the Peninsula Campaign and at Antietam. He was made major general on July 4, 1862 and commanded VI Corps at Chancellorsville and Gettysburg. His corps was largely used as a reserve at Gettysburg and suffered few casualties.

Slocum, Henry

(1827–1894)
Rank: Major General
Unit: XII Corps

Henry Slocum graduated from West Point in 1852 and practiced law before the Civil War. After being

ABOVE: Known as excessively deliberate and cautious, Henry Slocum was sometimes called "Slow Come."

wounded at First Manassas, he was made brigadier general on August 9, 1861. He commanded a brigade during the Peninsula Campaign and at Antietam. He was promoted to major general on July 4, 1862 and led XII Corps at Fredericksburg and Chancellorsville. He commanded the right wing of the Army of the Potomac at Gettysburg.

Stannard, George

(1820–1886)

Rank: Brigadier General

Unit: 3rd Brigade, 3rd Division, I Corps

George Stannard was a Vermont merchant and militiaman before the Civil War. He fought at First Manassas and was made brigadier general on March 11, 1863. He commanded a brigade at Gettysburg that delivered a lethal barrage of gunfire into the flank of Pickett's Charge. Observing the action, division commander Major General Abner Doubleday declared, "Glory to God, glory to God! See the Vermonters go it!"

Steinwehr, Adolph von

(1822–1877)

Rank: Brigadier General

Unit: 2nd Division, XI Corps

Adolph von Steinwehr was a Prussian military officer who immigrated to the United States, and, like Carl Schurz, was a "Latin Farmer." At the start of the Civil War, he raised a regiment, consisting primarily of German immigrants, which he commanded at First Manassas. He was promoted to brigadier general on October 12, 1861 and commanded a brigade in the Valley Campaign against Lieutenant General Stonewall Jackson. Steinwehr commanded a division at Chancellorsville and Gettysburg. On July 1, he was ordered by Major General Oliver

EXCERPT FROM STANNARD'S OFFICIAL REPORT OF HIS BRIGADE'S ACTIONS ON JULY 3

HDQRS. THIRD BRIG., THIRD DIV., FIRST ARMY CORPS,
Gettysburg, PA, July 4, 1863

Lieut. Col. C. KINGSBURY,
Jr., Assistant Adjutant-General

SIR:

At about 2:00 p.m. the enemy again commenced a vigorous attack upon my position. After subjecting us for one and one-half hours to the severest cannonade of the whole battle, from 100 guns or more, the enemy charged with a heavy column of infantry, at least one division, in close column by regiments. The charge was aimed directly upon my command, but owing apparently to the firm front shown them, the enemy diverged midway, and came upon the line on my right. But they did not thus escape the warm reception prepared for them by the Vermonters. During this charge the enemy suffered from the fire of the Thirteenth and Fourteenth, the range being short. At the commencement of the attack, I called the Sixteenth from the skirmish line, and placed them in close column by division in my immediate rear. As soon as the change of the point of attack became evident, I ordered a flank attack upon the enemy's column. Forming in the open meadow in front of our lines, the Thirteenth changed front forward on first company; the Sixteenth, after

deploying, performed the same, and formed on the left of the Thirteenth, at right angles to the main line of our army, bringing them in line of battle upon the flank of the charging division of the enemy, and opened a destructive fire at short range, which the enemy sustained but a very few moments before the larger portion of them surrendered and marched in—not as conquerors, but as captives.

I am, with much respect, your obedient servant,

GEO. J. STANNARD,
Brig. Gen. of Vols., Comdg. 3d Brig., 3d Div.,
1st A. C

LEFT: "Slow Trot" or "Tardy George" Sykes was not known for offensive action.

on September 21, 1861. He commanded a brigade during the Peninsula Campaign and at the battles of Antietam, Fredericksburg, and Chancellorsville. He was promoted to major general on November 29, 1862 and commanded the V Corps at Gettysburg. He had a reputation as being aggressive on the defense but lacking initiative when audacity was required.

Vincent, Strong

(1837–1863)
Rank: Colonel
Unit: 3rd Brigade, 1st Division, V Corps

Strong Vincent was promoted to colonel on June 27, 1862. He commanded the 3rd Brigade, 1st Division, V Corps at Gettysburg. He, with Colonel Joshua Chamberlain, held Little Round Top and saved the Federal flank from being rolled up during the second day's fighting. Admonishing his men, "Don't give an inch!" he was shot during the fierce fighting and died July 7; most likely without knowing he had been promoted to brigadier general on July 3.

BELOW: On the march to Gettysburg, Strong Vincent had written his pregnant wife, "If I fall, remember you have given your husband to the most righteous cause that ever widowed a woman."

Howard to secure Cemetery Hill, and this decision later provided a valuable rally point for the Federal line.

Sykes, George

(1822–1880)
Rank: Major General
Unit: V Corps

George Sykes graduated from West Point in 1842 and fought in the Seminole Wars and Mexican-American War. He fought at First Manassas and was appointed brigade general

Wadsworth, James

(1807–1864)
Rank: Brigadier General
Unit: 1st Division, I Corps

James Wadsworth was a lawyer before the Civil War. He served as a volunteer aide during First Manassas and was commissioned a brigadier general on August 9, 1861. He commanded a brigade before making an unsuccessful bid for governor of New York. Returning to the service, he commanded a division at Chancellorsville and Gettysburg.

Warren, Gouverneur

(1830–1882)
Rank: Major General
Unit: Chief of Engineers, Army of the Potomac

Gouverneur Warren graduated from West Point in 1850 and served as a topographical engineer for the U.S. Army before the Civil War. He commanded brigades during the Peninsula

LEFT: The son of a wealthy landowner, James Wadsworth was a Free Soil Republican.

Campaign and at Second Manassas and Antietam. He was promoted to brigadier general on September 26, 1862 and major general on May 3, 1863. As Chief Engineer of the Army of the Potomac, his keen eye for terrain identified the importance of Little Round Top on July 2 at Gettysburg. Seizing on

FACING PAGE: This photograph shows, from left to right: Gouverneur Warren, William H. French, Major General George Meade, Chief of Artillery Henry Hunt, Brigadier General Andrew Humphreys, and V Corps commander Major General George Sykes.

EXCERPT FROM WADSWORTH'S OFFICIAL REPORT OF HIS DIVISION'S FIGHTING ON JULY 1

HEADQUARTERS FIRST DIVISION, FIRST ARMY CORPS,
In the Field, near Gettysburg, PA., July 4, 1863

SIR:
At about 2:30 p.m. Major-General Schurz, who had been advanced on our right, fell back after partially engaging the enemy, and left our right exposed. The enemy advanced in large force from that direction, and on our left the Third Division of this corps was driven back. Finding myself outflanked on both right and left, heavily pressed in front, and my ammunition nearly exhausted, at 3:45 o'clock I ordered the command to retire. The movement was effected in good order, and all the artillery brought off safely, excepting one caisson, the Seventh Wisconsin bringing up the rear, and suffering heavily, with the whole of the command, from the fire from our front and both flanks.

The severity of the contest during the day will be indicated by the painful fact that at least half of the officers and men who went into the engagement were killed or wounded.

I have the honor to be, very respectfully, your obedient servant,

JAS. S. WADSWORTH,
Brigadier-General of Volunteers

EXCERPT FROM SYKES'S OFFICIAL REPORT OF WEED'S ACTIONS ON JULY 2—HEADQUARTERS FIFTH ARMY CORPS, CAMP NEAR WARRENTON, VA., JULY 31, 1863

Brig. Gen. S. WILLIAMS,
Assistant Adjutant-General, Army of the Potomac

SIR:

In the meantime Vincent's brigade, of this division, had seized the rocky height, closely followed by Weed's brigade, Second Division. These troops were posted under the direction of General Warren, chief engineer of this army. After closing the interval made by Birney with the brigades of General Barnes, I rode rapidly to the Taneytown pike to bring up the remaining troops of the corps, and on my return with them found the greater part of Weed's brigade moving away from the height where it had been stationed, and where its presence was vital. I dispatched a staff officer to know of the general why he had vacated the ground assigned him. His reply was, "By order of General Sickles." I at once directed him to reoccupy it, which was done at the double-quick step. Hardly had he reached it before the enemy came on in tremendous force. Vincent's brigade and O'Rorke's regiment (Weed's brigade) were and had been sorely pressed. Both those heroic commanders had fallen; but Weed again in position, Hazlett working his guns superbly, and the timely arrival of Ayres' brigades of regulars, who were at once ordered to attack, stemmed the tide, and rolled away the foe in our front.

At a later hour, by the withdrawal or retreat of the troops on his right—first, a division of the Third Corps, and next, Caldwell's command, of the Second Corps—a large body of the enemy gained his right and rear, and Ayres was compelled to fight his way, front and flank, to the heel of the gorge. This he did steadily, in excellent order, and connected with his left brigade (Weed's) on the general line of battle. But his loss was fearful; some of the regiments left 60 percent of their number on the ground. As Ayres assumed this new position, General Crawford's command (my Third Division) was ordered to the front, and, entering the woods, became briskly engaged with the enemy. This combat lasted till dusk, and resulted in General Crawford's gaining considerable ground, capturing many prisoners, and a flag of a Georgia regiment.

Night closed the fight. The key of the battle-field was in our possession intact. Vincent, Weed, and Hazlett, chiefs lamented throughout the corps and army, sealed with their lives the spot entrusted to their keeping, and on which so much depended. The general line of battle on the left was shortened, strengthened, firm. Pickets were established, and the troops slept on their arms. Sedgwick (Sixth Corps) had moved up to my aid.

I am, sir, respectfully, your obedient servant,

GEO. SYKES,
Major-General, Commanding Corps

the importance of the position, he rushed Colonel Strong Vincent's brigade to its defense in the nick of time, saving the Federal flank. An iconic statue of Warren with his binoculars in hand stands on Little Round Top. The inscription reads, "Led to this spot by his military sagacity on July 2, 1863, General Gouverneur Kemble Warren, then Chief Engineer of the Army of the Potomac, detected General Hood's flanking movement and by promptly assuming the responsibility of

ordering troops to this place saved the key of the Union position."

Weed, Stephen

(1834–1863)
Rank: Brigadier General
Unit: V Corps

Stephen Weed graduated from West Point in 1854 and fought in the Seminole Wars and in the West. He was in charge of an artillery battery during the Peninsula Campaign and at Antietam. He commanded all the artillery of V Corps at Fredericksburg and Chancellorsville. Weed was promoted from captain to brigade general on June 6, 1863. He was instrumental in the defense of Little Round Top and was killed there on July 2.

Webb, Alexander

(1835–1911)
Rank: Brigadier General
Unit: 2nd Brigade, 2nd Division, II Corps

Alexander Webb graduated from West Point in 1855. He served at First Manassas, during the Peninsula Campaign, at Antietam, and Chancellorsville. In spite of limited experience with troop command, he was promoted to

FACING PAGE: Alexander Webb received the Medal of Honor for gallantry in helping halt Armistead's Brigade during Pickett's Charge on July 3.

brigadier general on June 23, 1863 and placed in command of the 2nd Brigade in Major General John Gibbon's division of II Corps. Webb's brigade occupied the focal point of Pickett's Charge on the third day of Gettysburg. Webb was wounded in the fighting and awarded the Medal of Honor for his gallant defense.

Wright, Horatio

(1820–1899)
Rank: Major General
Unit: 1st Division, VI Corps

Horatio Wright graduated from West Point in 1841 and served as an engineer before the Civil War. He fought at First Manassas and during the Port Royal Expedition. He was promoted to brigadier general on September 14, 1861 and led a division at Secessionville. He was promoted to major general on July 18, 1862, but the Senate refused to ratify the promotion, and it was revoked. He led a division in Major General John Sedgwick's lightly engaged VI Corps at Gettysburg.

After the Civil War, Horatio Wright participated in the completion of the Washington Monument and construction of the Brooklyn Bridge.

Key Confederate Leaders

The Confederate leadership at Gettysburg centered on General Robert E. Lee. It was his success, vision, confidence, strategy, and credibility that brought the Army of Northern Virginia into Northern territory.

B ut Lee was now without his most trusted subordinate, Lieutenant General Stonewall Jackson, who had died in the costly victory at Chancellorsville. Thus Lee had to elevate to corps command lieutenant generals A. P. Hill and Richard Ewell, who were untested at that level. Lee would also be disappointed by some of his proven commanders. Lieutenant General

FACING PAGE: Generals Lee and Jeb Stuart review Confederate cavalry before the battle of Brandy Station, June 9, 1863.

RIGHT: It was Lee's leadership that provided the Confederate army with the confidence to launch successive invasions of the North, first in September 1862, and again in June 1863.

James Longstreet would be resistant to Lee's offensive strategy and Major General Jeb Stuart would fail to provide Lee the intelligence he so desperately needed. The hard fought Battle of Gettysburg took its toll on the Confederate leadership, and solid performers like Lewis Armistead, William Barksdale, and William Pender were among the casualties. Others, like George Pickett, survived the fighting and became forever associated with the battle. There would be many disadvantages to overcome when the Army of Northern Virginia launched the Gettysburg Campaign, and the Confederate leadership would have to turn in an extraordinary performance if it hoped to even the odds.

Alexander, Edward Porter

(1835–1910)

Rank: Chief of Artillery

Unit: Longstreet's Corps

Edward Porter Alexander graduated from the United Stated Military Academy at West Point in 1857. He was commissioned as an engineer and served as an instructor at West Point. In November 1862, Alexander was given command of an artillery battalion under Major General James Longstreet. He was promoted to colonel

in December and served at Fredericksburg and Chancellorsville. At Gettysburg he superintended the massive but ineffective artillery barrage that preceded Pickett's Charge. His book, *Military Memoirs of a Confederate*, published in 1907, remains a classic account of the overall Confederate effort.

LEFT: Edward Porter Alexander did the best he could to provide artillery support for Pickett's Charge, but it would not be enough.

EXCERPT FROM RICHARD ANDERSON'S REPORT OF HIS DIVISION'S ACTIONS AT GETTYSBURG

HDQRS. ANDERSON'S DIVISION, THIRD ARMY CORPS
Orange Court-House, VA, August 7, 1863

Maj. WILLIAM H. PALMER,
A. A. and I. G., and Chief of Staff, Third Army Corps

MAJOR:
The conduct of the troops under my command was in the highest degree praiseworthy and commendable throughout the campaign. Obedient to the orders of the commanding general, they refrained from taking into their own hands retaliation upon the enemy for the inhuman wrongs and outrages inflicted upon them in the wanton destruction of their property and homes. Peaceable inhabitants suffered no molestation.

In a land of plenty, they often suffered hunger and want. One-fourth of their number marched, ragged and barefooted, through towns in which it was well ascertained that the merchants had concealed supplies of clothing. In battle they lacked none of that courage and spirit which has ever distinguished the soldiers of the Army of Northern Virginia, and, if complete success did not attend their efforts, their failure cannot be laid upon their shortcoming, but must be recognized and accepted as the will and decree of the Almighty disposer of human affairs.

I am, very respectfully, your most obedient servant,

R. H. ANDERSON,
Major-General, Commanding Division

Anderson, George

(1824–1901)

Rank: Brigadier General

Unit: Anderson's Brigade

George "Tige" Anderson was a student at Emory College in Georgia when he left to serve in the Mexican-American War. Early in the Civil War, he fought during the Seven Days Battle, Second Manassas, and Antietam. He was appointed brigadier general on November 1, 1862 and fought at Fredericksburg and was part of the Suffolk Campaign. At Gettysburg, he commanded a brigade in Major General John Bell Hood's division. Anderson was severely wounded in the fighting at Devil's Den.

Anderson, Richard

(1821–1879)
Rank: Major General
Unit: Anderson's Division

Richard Anderson graduated from West Point in 1842 and served in the Mexican-American War. He was named brigadier general on July 18, 1861. He commanded a brigade during the Peninsula Campaign. He was promoted to major general on July 14, 1862 and commanded a division at Chancellorsville. His performance at Gettysburg, particularly on July 2, was relatively uninspired. An angry Brigadier General Cadmus Wilcox reported he was "quite certain that Gen'l A. never saw a foot of the ground on which his three brigades fought on the 2nd of July."

Archer, James

(1817–1864)
Rank: Brigadier General
Unit: Archer's Brigade

James Archer was a prewar lawyer and veteran of the Mexican-American War. He was

ABOVE: James Archer had the unfortunate distinction of being the first of Lee's general officers in the Army of Northern Virginia to be taken prisoner.

appointed brigadier general on June 3, 1862 and fought with Major General John Bell Hood's Texas brigade from the Peninsula Campaign through Chancellorsville. At Gettysburg he commanded a brigade in Major General Henry Heth's division. Archer was captured with a large part of his command on July 1 and not exchanged until the summer of 1864. By the time of his release, he was in poor health and died soon after.

Armistead, Lewis

(1817–1863)
Rank: Brigadier General
Unit: Armistead's Brigade

Lewis Armistead attended West Point but did not graduate. He served with distinction in Mexico, winning two brevets and helping storm the citadel at Chapultepec. He resigned from the U.S. Army on May 26, 1861 and was commissioned a major in the Confederate army. By April 1, 1862 Armistead was a brigadier general, and he commanded his brigade from the Peninsula Campaign to Gettysburg. He is most famous for his role in Pickett's Charge on the third day of the Battle of Gettysburg. Cheering his brigade forward with his hat on his sword, Armistead briefly reached the Federal lines commanded by his old army friend Winfield Scott Hancock. Armistead was mortally wounded in the attack, but the position he reached is commemorated as the "High Water Mark of the Confederacy."

Barksdale, William

(1821–1863)
Rank: Brigadier General
Unit: Barksdale's Brigade

William Barksdale retired from Congress on January 12, 1861 when Mississippi seceded. He then served as quartermaster general of the

Mississippi army until he entered the Confederate army as colonel of the 13th Mississippi Regiment. He commanded the regiment at First Manassas and during the Peninsula Campaign until he was given a brigade on June 29, 1862. "Barksdale's Brigade" consisted of the 13th, 17th, 18th, and 21st Mississippi regiments. He fought at Fredericksburg, Antietam, Chancellorsville, and Gettysburg, where he was mortally wounded. As he lay dying he reportedly said, "Tell my wife I am shot, but we fought like hell."

Benning, Henry

(1814–1875)
Rank: Brigadier General
Unit: Benning's Brigade

A lawyer before the Civil War, Henry Benning commanded a Georgia regiment during the Peninsula Campaign and at Second Manassas and a brigade at Antietam and Fredericksburg. He was made brigadier general on April 23, 1863. At Gettysburg, he commanded a brigade in Major General John Bell Hood's division.

Davis, Jefferson

(1808–1889)
President of the CSA

Jefferson Davis graduated from West Point in 1828 and served in the dragoons for seven years. He won national fame during the Mexican-American War for his heroics at the Battle of Buena Vista, where his 1st Mississippi Rifles halted a Mexican cavalry charge and prevented an American defeat. He then served in the U.S. Senate and as Secretary of War under President

LEFT: Hard-charging William Barksdale had a reputation for always being where the fighting was thickest.

RIGHT: As president of the Confederacy, Jefferson Davis faced the difficult task of building a fledgling nation in the midst of a war.

ABOVE: Jubal Early helped spark decades of controversy in shaping Gettysburg's memory within the Lost Cause.

Franklin Pierce. He was an able Secretary of War and helped prod the army into adopting the Springfield Model 1855 rifled musket.

Davis served in the Senate until Mississippi seceded in January 1861. In February, he was chosen to be President of the Confederate States of America. Despite his political and military experience, Davis proved to be a much less effective commander-in-chief than his seemingly less qualified Federal counterpart, Abraham Lincoln.

Davis did enjoy an effective relationship with General Robert E. Lee, both when Lee was

Davis's military adviser and later as the commander of the Army of Northern Virginia. However, Davis is accused of being too beholden to Lee's Virginia-centric strategic views and ignoring the western theater. Critics claim it was for this reason that Davis agreed to Lee's plan to invade Northern territory in the summer of 1863 rather than reinforcing Vicksburg.

Early, Jubal

(1816–1894)
Rank: Major General
Unit: Early's Division

Jubal Early graduated from West Point in 1837 and received a commission in the 3rd U.S. Artillery. He served as a brigade commander at First Manassas and was subsequently promoted to brigadier general. During the Peninsula Campaign, he entered into an argument with Major General James Longstreet about the conduct of the Battle of Williamsburg, and a feud between the two developed. The tension continued long after the battle as Early championed the generalship of General Robert E. Lee at Longstreet's expense. Early led a division at Gettysburg. After the war, he went to Mexico and then Canada before returning to Lynchburg, Virginia to practice law. As president

RIGHT: Richard Ewell had the appropriate nickname "Old Baldy." By the time of Gettysburg he had had his leg amputated and replaced by a wooden one.

of the Southern Historical Society, he vociferously defended Lee's actions at Gettysburg, remaining vehemently anti-Longstreet in the process.

Ewell, Richard

(1817–1872)
Rank: Lieutenant General
Unit: II Army Corps

Richard "Dick" Ewell graduated from West Point in 1840 and served in the West and in Mexico. He commanded a brigade at First Manassas and was promoted to major general on January 23, 1862. When General Robert E. Lee reorganized

the Army of Northern Virginia after Lieutenant General Stonewall Jackson's death, Ewell was promoted to lieutenant general on May 23, 1863 and elevated to corps command. Bold and wily as a division commander, Ewell had difficulty transitioning to the corps level. His failure to act on Lee's discretionary order to capture Cemetery Hill on the first day at Gettysburg allowed the Federals to strengthen their line.

Garnett, Richard

(1817–1863)
Rank: Brigadier General
Unit: Garnett's Brigade

Richard Garnett graduated from West Point in 1841 and fought in the Seminole Wars. On November 14, 1861 he was appointed brigadier general. He was placed under arrest by Lieutenant General Stonewall Jackson for withdrawing his brigade at Kernstown during the Shenandoah Valley Campaign. He was later released but remained deeply troubled by the incident. He commanded brigades at Antietam and Fredericksburg and participated in the Suffolk Campaign.

At Gettysburg he was killed during Pickett's Charge in what many considered an attempt to correct the slight to his reputation Garnett felt he suffered at Kernstown.

RIGHT: After the Civil War, John Brown Gordon served as Governor of Georgia.

Excerpt From Capt. H. Owen's **Philadelphia Weekly Press** *Account of Pickett's Charge. Owen Served In Garnett's Brigade*
The command now came along the line, "Front, forward!" and the column resumed its direction straight down upon the center of the enemy's position. The destruction of life in the ranks of that advancing host was fearful beyond precedent, officers going down by dozens and the men by scores and fifties.

Gordon, John Brown

(1832–1904)
Rank: Brigadier General
Unit: Gordon's Brigade

John Brown Gordon left the University of Georgia to become a lawyer and later worked as a superintendent of a coal mine. Although he had no previous military training at the time of the Civil War, he was elected captain of a volunteer company known as the "Raccoon Roughs." He was later sent to Virginia and fought in the Peninsula Campaign. Gordon was seriously wounded in the head at Antietam, but recovered and was promoted to brigadier general on November 1, 1862. He commanded a brigade at Gettysburg. After the war, he was instrumental in the affairs of the United Confederate Veterans and served as its first commander-in-chief from 1890 until his death in 1904. In his autobiography,

LEFT: Wade Hampton was active at Brandy Station and the cavalry charge on the third day at Gettysburg.

Reminiscences of the Civil War, he weighed in on the "sunrise attack" controversy opining, "General Lee distinctly ordered Longstreet to attack early the morning of the second day, and if he had done so, two of the largest corps of Meade's army would not have been in the fight; but Longstreet delayed the attack until four o'clock in the afternoon, and thus lost his opportunity of occupying Little Round Top, the key to the position, which he might have done in the morning without firing a shot or losing a man."

Hampton, Wade

(1818–1902)
Rank: Brigadier General
Unit: Hampton's Brigade

Wade Hampton was one of the South's wealthiest planters and bastions of the Southern aristocracy. In spite of his social position, he doubted the economy of the slave labor system and did not favor secession. He was one of the Confederacy's most dashing and bold cavalrymen, being wounded three times during the Battle of Gettysburg alone. He joined Richard Taylor and Nathan Bedford Forrest as one of only three Confederates to reach the rank of lieutenant general without any formal military training.

Harrison, Henry Thomas

(1832–1923)
Spy

Usually referred to simply as "Harrison," Henry Thomas Harrison was Lieutenant General James Longstreet's favorite spy. Longstreet had first employed Harrison's services during the Suffolk Campaign in April 1863 after being introduced to him by Secretary of War James Seddon. Longstreet's chief of staff Brigadier General Moxley Sorrell described Harrison as "altogether an extraordinary character," but Harrison remains a shadowy and mysterious figure. With the absence of Major General Jeb Stuart's cavalry at Gettysburg, Harrison's reports became one of the few sources of intelligence available to the Confederates. On June 28, 1863, he informed Longstreet that the Federal forces were located around Frederick, Maryland and advancing north, and that Major General George Meade had replaced Joseph Hooker as commander of the Army of the Potomac.

Heth, Henry

(1825–1899)
Rank: Major General
Unit: Heth's Division

Henry Heth graduated from West Point in 1847 and served in the Mexican-American War. He was appointed brigadier general on January 6,

ABOVE: Both Jackson and Lee reportedly spoke of Ambrose Powell Hill on their death beds. Jackson said, "Order A. P. Hill to prepare for action," and Lee, although it is a matter of some dispute, commanded, "Tell Hill he must come up!"

1862. General Robert E. Lee brought him to the Army of Northern Virginia in January 1863 where he served as brigade commander. Heth was promoted to major general on May 24, 1863 and commanded a division at Gettysburg. He was instrumental in the first day's battle but was wounded, and Brigadier General James Pettigrew commanded his division for Pickett's Charge. Heth had been struck by a bullet in the head, but he was wearing an oversized hat stuffed with several rolled-up sheets of paper to improve the fit. The bullet fractured his skull and rendered him unconscious, but the absorptive qualities of the paper padding is credited with saving his life.

Hill, Ambrose Powell

(1825–1865)
Rank: Lieutenant General
Unit: III Army Corps

Ambrose Powell (A. P.) Hill graduated from West Point in 1847. Prior to the Civil War, he served in the Mexican-American War, the Seminole Wars, on the frontier, and for almost five years in the Office of the Superintendent of the United States Coast Survey. He was promoted to major general on May 26, 1862 and figured prominently during the Peninsula and Seven Days campaigns as a division commander. He emerged with a reputation as a combative, if not reckless, fighter. He also had a petulant personality that led to difficult relationships with Lieutenant General James Longstreet and Lieutenant General Stonewall Jackson.

When Lee reorganized the Army of Northern Virginia after Jackson's death, Hill was given command of the newly created III Corps which he led at Gettysburg. He was ill during the battle, and his performance there lacked the aggressiveness Hill had shown elsewhere.

Hood, John Bell

(1831–1879)
Rank: Major General
Unit: Hood's Division

John Bell Hood graduated from West Point in 1853. He was wounded in Indian fighting before resigning from the army in April 1861. On March 6, 1862, he was appointed brigadier general and given command of the "Texas Brigade." During the Peninsula Campaign, he launched a desperate final charge that broke

ABOVE: Hood and his staff pose for a photograph somewhere in Atlanta.
LEFT: At Gettysburg, John Bell Hood showed his characteristic combativeness during the fighting for Devil's Den.

the Federal line at Gaines's Mill. On the strength of that performance, Hood's Texans became General Robert E. Lee's favorite shock troops. The bold attack also demonstrated

John Imboden missed much of the fighting at Gettysburg, but was instrumental in safeguarding the Confederate withdrawal.

Hood's temperament as an aggressive, offensive-minded officer.

Hood continued to command the brigade at Second Manassas and Antietam until he was promoted to major general on October 10 and given a division in Lieutenant General James Longstreet's Corps. A bad wound at Gettysburg resulted in a crippled left arm.

Imboden, John

(1823–1895)
Rank: Brigadier General
Unit: Imboden's Brigade

John Imboden was a lawyer and legislator in Virginia. Before the war he organized the Staunton Artillery, which he commanded at First Manassas. He then organized the 1st Partisan Rangers and fought at Cross Keys and Port Republic. He was promoted to brigadier general on January 28, 1863.

In April and May 1863, Imboden conducted a raid into northwestern Virginia, which cut the Baltimore and Ohio Railroad and captured several thousand horses and cattle. He conducted screening operations during the Gettysburg Campaign and was given the difficult task of leading the withdrawal of the wounded and wagon trains back to Virginia after the battle.

ABOVE: **Edward Johnson helped defeat the Federal force at Winchester as the Army of Northern Virginia advanced north toward Gettysburg.**

Johnson, Edward

(1816–1873)
Rank: Major General
Unit: Johnson's Division

Edward "Allegheny" Johnson graduated from West Point in 1838 and fought in the Seminole Wars and Mexican-American War. He performed admirably during the Shenandoah Valley Campaign in 1862. He was promoted to major general on February 28, 1863 and commanded Lieutenant General Stonewall Jackson's old division at Gettysburg.

Jones, William

(1824–1864)
Rank: Brigadier General
Unit: Laurel Brigade

William "Grumble" Jones graduated from West Point in 1848 and served in the West until resigning in 1857 to farm. In May 1861 he was commissioned a major in the Virginia cavalry. He served at Cedar Mountain, Groveton, Second Manassas, and in northern North Carolina, and was made brigadier general on September 19, 1862. He conducted screening operations during the Gettysburg Campaign, but a disagreement with Major General Jeb Stuart led to Jones's reassignment to command of the Department of Southwest Virginia and East Tennessee.

Kemper, James

(1823–1895)
Rank: Brigadier General
Unit: Kemper's Brigade

James Kemper was a lawyer and veteran of the Mexican-American War. He was appointed brigadier general on June 3, 1862 and led a brigade during the Seven Days Campaign and at Antietam and Fredericksburg. He was seriously wounded during Pickett's Charge, captured, and subsequently exchanged. His wounds were severe enough to preclude further service in the field but he was promoted to major general on September 19, 1864 and served in administrative positions.

Kershaw, Joseph

(1822–1894)
Rank: Brigadier General
Unit: Kershaw's Brigade

Joseph Kershaw was a South Carolina lawyer and Mexican-American War veteran. He was appointed brigadier general on February 13, 1862 and commanded a brigade from the

Peninsula Campaign through Gettysburg. Although not trained as a professional soldier, he proved capable in battle.

Lane, James

(1833–1907)
Rank: Brigadier General
Unit: Lane's Brigade

James Lane graduated from the Virginia Military Institute in 1854 and won early renown for his participation in the Battle of Big Bethel. He was wounded during the Peninsula Campaign, fought at Second Manassas, and commanded a brigade at Antietam. He was appointed brigadier general on November 1, 1862 and commanded a brigade at Fredericksburg and Chancellorsville. At Gettysburg his brigade was actively engaged on the first and third days' fighting, suffering almost 50 percent casualties.

Law, Evander

(1836–1920)
Rank: Brigadier General
Unit: Law's Brigade

Evander Law graduated from The Military College of South Carolina (also known as The Citadel) in 1856. He fought at First Manassas,

LEFT: Joseph Kershaw commanded a brigade in McLaws's division of Longstreet's Corps at Gettysburg.

was a regimental commander during the Peninsula Campaign, Second Manassas, and Antietam. Law was appointed brigadier general on October 2, 1862. He led his Alabama brigade in the unsuccessful attack on Little Round Top on the second day at Gettysburg. He assumed command of the division after Major General John Bell Hood was wounded.

EXCERPT FROM LANE'S OFFICIAL REPORT OF HIS BRIGADE'S ACTIONS AT GETTYSBURG ON JULY 3

HEADQUARTERS LANE'S BRIGADE
August 13, 1863

Maj. JOSEPH A. ENGELHARD,
Assistant Adjutant-General, Pender's Light Division

MAJOR:
Now in command of my own brigade, I moved forward to the support of Pettigrew's right, through the woods in which our batteries were planted, and through all open field about a mile, in full view of the enemy's fortified position, and under a murderous artillery and infantry fire.

As soon as Pettigrew's command gave back, Lowrance's brigade and my own, without ever having halted, took position on the left of the troops which were still contesting the ground with the enemy. My command never moved forward more handsomely. The men reserved their fire, in accordance with orders, until within good range of the enemy, and then opened with telling effect, repeatedly driving the cannoneers from their pieces, completely silencing the guns in our immediate front, and breaking the line of infantry which was formed on the crest of the hill. We advanced to within a few yards of the stone wall, exposed all the while to a heavy raking artillery fire from the right. My left was here very much exposed, and a column of the enemy's infantry was thrown forward in that direction, which enfiladed my whole line. This forced me to withdraw my brigade, the troops on my right having already done so. We fell back as well as could be expected, reformed immediately in rear of the artillery, as directed by General Trimble, and remained there until the following morning.

I cannot speak in too high terms of the behavior of my brigade in this bloody engagement. Both officers and men moved forward with a heroism unsurpassed, giving the brigade inspector and his rear guard nothing to do.

Our great loss tells but too sadly of the gallant bearing of my command—660 out of an effective total of 1,355, including ambulance corps and rear guard, our loss on the 1st and 2nd being but slight.

Respectfully,
J. H. LANE, Brigadier General

Lee, Fitzhugh
(1835–1905)
Rank: Brigadier General
Unit: F. Lee's Brigade

Fitzhugh Lee graduated from West Point in 1856. He performed admirably during the Peninsula Campaign and was made brigadier general on July 24, 1862. He commanded a brigade in Major General Jeb Stuart's cavalry and was considered by many to be Stuart's favorite officer.

Lee, Robert E.
(1807–1870)
Rank: General
Unit: Army of Northern Virginia

Robert Edward Lee graduated second in the West Point class of 1829 and distinguished himself during the Mexican-American War as an engineer. After Virginia seceded from the Union, Lee resigned his commission and took command of the Virginia land and naval forces until they were incorporated in the Confederate States. He was subsequently appointed a brigadier general in the Confederate army and attained the rank of full general on August 7, 1861. After an unsuccessful campaign in western Virginia and supervising coastal defenses in Georgia and the Carolinas, Lee was named the military adviser to President Jefferson Davis.

Lee replaced General Joseph Johnston as field commander on May 31, 1862 after Johnston was wounded at Seven Pines. This event changed the course of the war. In contrast to the strained relationship between Johnston and Davis, Lee and Davis enjoyed a smooth-working communication and collaboration. Even more significantly, Lee exchanged Johnston's largely defensive strategy for an audacious offensive-defensive strategy that would seize the initiative and dictate the timing and tempo of operations. Lee successfully repulsed Major General George McClellan on the Virginia Peninsula and then seized the initiative by decimating Major General John Pope's forces at Second Manassas. During the Peninsula Campaign and Second Manassas, Lee and Lieutenant General Stonewall Jackson developed a synergistic relationship that brought out the best in both men. Lee preferred to give the broad, discretionary orders on which Jackson thrived, and Jackson was able to efficiently put Lee's intent into action.

Building on the victory at Second Manassas, Lee launched the Antietam Campaign, his first invasion on Northern territory. After the battle ended in a tactical draw, Lee was forced to return to Virginia. The campaign did indicate Lee's overwhelming confidence in his army and his firm belief in the offensive, characteristics that perhaps did not serve him in good stead given the Confederacy's scant resources.

LEFT: Robert E. Lee took responsibility for the defeat at Gettysburg, stating, "It's all my fault."

The disparity between Lee's army and his Federal counterpart made the strategy of defense a better option for the Army of Northern Virginia, and Lee proved this at the Battle of Fredericksburg on December 13, 1862. More to Lee's liking, however, was his brilliant offensive victory at Chancellorsville on May 4, 1863 in which he teamed with Jackson for what has been called "Lee's masterpiece." However, Lee was

ABOVE: Before the Civil War, William Henry Fitzhugh Lee served in the famed 6th Infantry commanded by Albert Sidney Johnston.

frustrated with his inability to completely destroy his enemy, and the battle showed his fixation with the offensive.

Chancellorsville was a costly victory for Lee because he lost Jackson. Lee was then forced to reorganize his army into three corps, because he did not have a subordinate strong enough to replace Jackson. Lee sorely missed Jackson during the Battle of Gettysburg, lamenting afterward, "If I [would have] had Stonewall Jackson at Gettysburg, I would have won that fight." Instead, Lee lost 20,000 men, which, along with the earlier loss of Jackson, forever blunted Lee's offensive capability.

Lee, William Henry Fitzhugh

(1837–1891)
Rank: Brigadier General
Unit: W. H. F. Lee's Brigade

"Rooney" Lee was the second son of General Robert E. Lee. He served in Major General Jeb Stuart's cavalry during the ride around Major General George McClellan's army. Lee was wounded at Turner's Gap during the Antietam Campaign, but recovered in time for the Chambersburg Raid of October 1862. Lee was appointed brigadier general on September 15, 1862. He fought at Fredericksburg and Chancellorsville and was severely wounded at Brandy Station. Colonel John Chambliss commanded the brigade while Lee recovered.

Longstreet, James

(1821–1904)
Rank: Lieutenant General
Unit: I Army Corps

James Longstreet graduated from West Point in 1842 and then served in Florida and Mexico where he was often in the thick of serious combat. During the Civil War, Longstreet showed a marked penchant for the defense, and some observers have explained this characteristic as a reaction to his personal experience with the high cost of frontal attacks in Mexico. After noteworthy performances at First Manassas, during the Peninsula Campaign, at Second Manassas, and at Antietam, he was promoted to lieutenant general on October 9, 1862.

At Fredericksburg, Longstreet performed well in the type of defensive situation he favored. Long desiring an independent command, Longstreet was sent to Suffolk where he commanded the Department of North Carolina and Southern Virginia. During this unremarkable posting, Longstreet missed the great offensive battle at Chancellorsville.

After Longstreet rejoined the Army of Northern Virginia, he voiced passionate arguments against General Robert E. Lee's Gettysburg Campaign. Longstreet first attempted to persuade Lee to stay on the defensive in Virginia, and reinforce General Braxton Bragg around Chattanooga. When Lee remained adamant about invading Northern territory,

ABOVE: James Longstreet was lackluster at Gettysburg and became the central figure in the battle's controversy after the war.

Longstreet urged him to assume a tactical defensive position on ground that threatened Baltimore, Maryland or Washington, D.C. Unable to convince Lee of his point of view, Longstreet was uncommitted at Gettysburg, especially on the second day of the battle.

After the war, Longstreet fell out of favor with many Southerners because he joined the Republican Party. His criticism of Lee's strategy at Gettysburg also alienated him from many of

Lee's supporters, even though Lee affectionately called Longstreet his "Old War Horse."

Mahone, William

(1826–1895)
Rank: Brigadier General
Unit: Mahone's Brigade

William Mahone graduated from the Virginia Military Institute in 1847. He was made a brigadier general on November 16, 1861. He fought in all the major battles with the Army of Northern Virginia and was promoted to major general on July 30, 1864 as a result of his exemplary action at the Battle of the Crater. Mahone commanded a brigade at Gettysburg, but showed none of the aggressive fighting spirit that characterized his service elsewhere.

McLaws, Lafayette

(1821–1897)
Rank: Major General
Unit: McLaw's Division

Lafayette McLaws graduated from West Point in 1842 and served in Mexico, in the West, and on the Utah Expedition. He resigned from the U.S. Army on May 10, 1861 and was appointed brigadier general in the Confederate army on September 25. He fought during the Peninsula Campaign and was promoted to major general on May 23, 1862. McLaws served as

RIGHT: At just five feet, six inches tall, William Mahone was known as "Little Billy" or the "Bantam."

wounded at Chancellorsville but refused to leave the field. Pender was promoted to major general on May 27, 1863 and commanded a division at Gettysburg. He was severely wounded in the leg on the second day. The wound became infected and the leg had to be amputated. Pender never

LEFT: Lafayette McLaws was married to Emily Allison Taylor, a niece of President Zachary Taylor and cousin of Jefferson Davis.

BELOW: Of William Pender, Lee wrote, "His promise and usefulness as an officer were only equaled by the purity and excellence of his private life."

recovered and died on July 18. Just 29 years old, his death deprived the Confederacy of one of its most talented young generals.

Excerpt From Pender's Letter To His Wife Fanny, June 1863

I do not think we shall have much severe fighting this summer. We will get North for a few months but we shall have to come back by September or Oct. for their force will be increasing while ours will be decreasing, but by that time we shall probably give them such a taste of war, that they may be willing to say quit.

Pender's Dying Words, July 18, 1863

Tell my wife that I do not fear to die. I can confidently resign my soul to God, trusting in the atonement of Jesus Christ. My only regret is to leave her and our two children. I have always tried to do my duty in every sphere in which Providence has placed me.

a division commander at Harper's Ferry, Antietam, Fredericksburg, Chancellorsvile, and Gettysburg.

Pender, William

(1834–1863)
Rank: Major General
Unit: Pender's Division

William Pender graduated from West Point in 1854 and was promoted to brigadier general on June 3, 1862 after a solid performance at Seven Pines. He then fought at Second Manassas, Antietam, and Fredericksburg. He was thrice

Pendleton, William

(1809–1883)
Rank: Chief of Artillery
Unit: Army of Northern Virginia

William Pendleton graduated from West Point in 1830 and was ordained as an Episcopal minister in 1838. He was promoted to brigadier general on March 26, 1862 and became General Robert E. Lee's chief of artillery. After the

ABOVE: Showing considerable signs of wear and tear, this tunic is reputedly that worn by Pendleton.

reorganization of the Army of Northern Virginia in 1863, the general artillery reserve was broken up and the guns distributed to divisions and corps, but Pendleton retained his title as chief of artillery. Pendleton enjoyed a close friendship with Lee but had little impact as an artilleryman.

Pettigrew, James

(1828–1863)
Rank: Brigadier General
Unit: Pettigrew's Division

James Pettigrew was a prewar lawyer who assisted in the Confederate capture of Fort Sumter. He was commissioned brigadier general on February 26, 1862 and was wounded and captured during the Peninsula Campaign. He commanded a brigade in Major General Henry Heth's division at Gettysburg and commanded the division after Heth was wounded. Although the attack is commonly known as "Pickett's Charge," Pettigrew's division was the left unit on the Confederate line and was actively involved. During the Army of Northern Virginia's

EXCERPT FROM PENDLETON'S OFFICIAL REPORT OF THE ARTILLERY EXCHANGE ON JULY 3

HDQRS. ARTILLERY CORPS, ARMY OF NORTHERN VIRGINIA
September 12, 1863

General R. E. LEE,
Commanding

GENERAL:
At length, about 1:00 p.m., on the concerted signal, our guns in position, nearly 150, opened fire along the entire line from right to left, salvos by battery being much practiced, as directed, to secure greater deliberation and power. The enemy replied with their full force. So mighty an artillery contest has perhaps never been waged, estimating together the number and character of guns and the duration of the conflict. The average distance between contestants was about 1,400 yards, and the effect was necessarily serious on both sides. With the enemy, there was advantage of elevation

and protection from earthworks; but his fire was unavoidably more or less divergent, while ours was convergent. His troops were massed, ours diffused. We, therefore, suffered apparently much less. Great commotion was produced in his ranks, and his batteries were to such extent driven off or silenced as to have ensured his defeat but for the extraordinary strength of his position.

I have the honor to be, general, respectfully, your obedient servant,

W. N. PENDLETON,
Brigadier General, and Chief of Artillery

withdrawal after the battle, Pettigrew commanded a portion of the rear guard. He was mortally wounded on July 14 at Falling Waters, Maryland.

Pickett, George

(1825–1875)
Rank: Major General
Unit: Pickett's Division

George Pickett graduated last in the West Point class of 1846. He served in Mexico, winning some distinction carrying the 8th Infantry colors over the ramparts to victory at Chapultepec. He later served on the Texas frontier. He was a

LEFT: Pettigrew commanded Heth's division after the latter was wounded.

RIGHT: When asked why his charge failed, George Pickett quipped: "I've always thought the Yankees had something to do with it."

captain when he resigned from the U.S. Army on June 25, 1861 and was commissioned a colonel in the Confederate army. He was promoted to brigadier general on February 13, 1862 and fought well during the Peninsula Campaign until he was severely wounded in the shoulder at Gaines's Mill. He was promoted to major general on October 11 and commanded the Confederate center at Fredericksburg.

Pickett is best remembered for his association with the fateful charge on the third day of the Battle of Gettysburg. Pickett's division was repulsed amidst enormous casualties. The defeat left Pickett bitter, especially toward General Robert E. Lee, and Pickett's generalship after Gettysburg was unremarkable. He died in relative poverty, still distraught over his defeat at Gettysburg, but just as assuredly famous for it.

Posey, Carnot

(1813–1863)
Rank: Brigadier General
Unit: Posey's Brigade

Carnot Posey served with Jefferson Davis in Mexico. He was made brigadier general on November 1, 1862 and led a brigade at Fredericksburg, Chancellorsville, and Gettysburg. He died of wounds sustained at the Battle of Bristoe Station.

Rodes, Robert

(1829–1864)
Rank: Major General
Unit: Rodes's Division

Robert Rodes graduated from the Virginia Military Institute in 1848. He fought at First Manassas and was commissioned brigadier general on October 21, 1861. He was wounded during the Peninsula Campaign and fought well at Antietam and Chancellorsville. Rodes was promoted to major general on May 7, 1863. He commanded a division at Gettysburg, but his performance there did not live up to his earlier standards.

Steuart, George

(1828–1903)
Rank: Brigadier General
Unit: Steuart's Brigade

George "Maryland" Steuart graduated from West Point in 1848. He fought at First Manassas and was appointed brigadier general on March 6, 1862. At Gettysburg, he commanded a brigade in Major General Edward Johnson's division. He dismounted and kissed the ground of his native state when the Army of Northern Virginia crossed the Potomac River into Maryland. He reportedly "strongly disapproved of making the assault" on Culp's Hill on July 3, and bemoaned, "My poor boys! My poor boys!" when it failed.

Stuart, James Ewell Brown

(1833–1864)
Rank: Major General
Unit: Stuart's Division

James Ewell Brown "Jeb" Stuart graduated from West Point in 1850. He was promoted to brigadier general on September 24, 1861, and he commanded a cavalry brigade during the Peninsula Campaign, where he helped cover the Confederate retreat to Williamsburg on May 4, 1862.

From June 12 to June 15, Stuart rode entirely around Major General George McClellan's army. Returning to a hero's welcome, Stuart told General Robert E. Lee that the Federal right flank was vulnerable, information which helped set up the Battle of Mechanicsville. Stuart later brought Lee indications that McClellan had abandoned his offensive and was beginning to withdraw. He was promoted to major general on July 25, 1862.

Another of Stuart's intelligence triumphs occurred at Chancellorsville where he reported that Major General Joseph Hooker's flank was "in the air," setting up Lieutenant General Stonewall Jackson's famous flank attack. In actions such as these, Stuart's cavalry provided the Confederates with an excellent

RIGHT: **James Ewell Brown Stuart was one of several subordinates who failed Lee at Gettysburg.**

EXCERPT FROM WILCOX'S OFFICIAL REPORT OF HIS BRIGADE'S ACTIONS AT GETTYSBURG

HEADQUARTERS WILCOX'S BRIGADE,
Bunker Hill, VA, July 17, 1863

Maj. THOMAS S. MILLS,
Assistant Adjutant-General

SIR:

With reference to the action of the 3rd instant, I beg to report that early in the morning, before sunrise, the brigade was ordered out to support artillery under the command of Colonel Alexander, this artillery being placed along the Emmitsburg turnpike, and on ground won from the enemy the day before. My men had had nothing to eat since the morning of the 2nd, and had confronted and endured the dangers and fatigues of that day. They nevertheless moved to the front to the support of the artillery, as ordered. The brigade was formed in line parallel to the Emmitsburg turnpike and about 200 yards from it, artillery being in front, much of it on the road, and extending far beyond either flank of the brigade. My men occupied this position till about

3:20 p.m. Our artillery opened fire upon the enemy's artillery, and upon ground supposed to be occupied by his infantry. This fire was responded to promptly by the enemy's artillery, and continued with the greatest vivacity on either side for about one hour. In no previous battle of the war had we so much artillery engaged, and the enemy seemed not to be inferior in quantity.

During all this fire, my men were exposed to the solid shot and shell of the enemy, but suffered comparatively little, probably less than a dozen men killed and wounded. The brigade lying on my right (Kemper's) suffered severely. Our artillery ceased to fire after about one hour. The enemy continued to fire for awhile after ours had ceased. I do not believe a single battery of the enemy had been disabled so as to stop its fire.

I am, sir, very respectfully, your obedient servant,

C. M. WILCOX,
Brigadier General, Commanding, &c.

BELOW: Cadmus Wilcox was part of Professor Dennis Hart Mahan's "Napoleon Club" at West Point.

reconnaissance capability and gave Lee a marked intelligence advantage over his opponents, who had no equivalent to Stuart. Stuart was skilled not just at obtaining information. He also had a great knack for interpreting what he saw and providing Lee

with a perceptive intelligence summation.

Although Stuart's greatest utility was in gathering intelligence, he fought in the war's largest cavalry battle at Brandy Station, Virginia on June 9, 1863. The battle confirmed to the Federals that Lee was moving north for his Gettysburg Campaign, and Stuart was criticized for his performance in the Southern press. Some see Stuart's ill-advised Gettysburg raid as an effort to restore his reputation after this setback. Stuart set out on this ride on June 24 and did not return to Lee until July 2, forcing Lee to fight the Battle of Gettysburg without knowledge of the Federal dispositions. After this poor showing, Stuart fought at the Battle of the Wilderness and in Spotsylvania, before being mortally wounded on May 11, 1864 at the Battle of Yellow Tavern.

Trimble, Isaac

(1802–1888)
Rank: Major General
Unit: II Army Corps

Isaac Trimble graduated from West Point in 1822 and served as a railroad engineer and superintendent before the war. He was made brigadier general on August 9, 1861 and was severely wounded at Second Manassas. He was promoted to major general on April 23, 1863. At Gettysburg, he first served as aide to Lieutenant General Richard Ewell, and Ewell refused his request to lead an attack on Culp's Hill on July 1. Casualties in the Confederate command elevated him to command of the trail division during Pickett's Charge. Aggressive, but

unfamiliar with the brigades he commanded, Trimble's attack was ineffective. He was struck in the leg, and it had to be amputated. Unable to withdraw with the Army of Northern Virginia across the Potomac, he was captured and not exchanged until February 1865.

Wilcox, Cadmus

(1824–1890)
Rank: Brigadier General
Unit: Wilcox's Brigade

Cadmus Wilcox graduated from West Point in 1846 and served in Mexico. He was made brigadier general on October 21, 1861 and led a brigade from the Peninsula Campaign to Gettysburg. He lost 577 men on the second day and was unenthusiastic about his participation in Pickett's Charge. During that attack, he concluded "knowing that my small force could do nothing save to make a useless sacrifice of themselves, I ordered them back."

Wright, Ambrose

(1826–1872)
Rank: Brigadier General
Unit: Wright's Brigade

A Georgia lawyer and politician before the war, Ambrose Wright was made brigadier general on June 3, 1862. He commanded a brigade during the Peninsula Campaign and at Second

ABOVE: Ambrose Wright was part of a commission that tried unsuccessfully to persuade Maryland to secede from the Union.

Manassas, Antietam, Fredericksburg, Chancellorsville, and Gettysburg. Surveying the objective of Pickett's Charge, he astutely told Colonel Edward Porter Alexander, "Well, Alexander, it is mostly a question of supports. It is not as hard to get there as it looks. I was there yesterday with my brigade. The real difficulty is to stay there after you get there—for the whole infernal Yankee army is up there in a bunch!"

ORDER OF BATTLE: UNITED STATES ARMY (UNION)

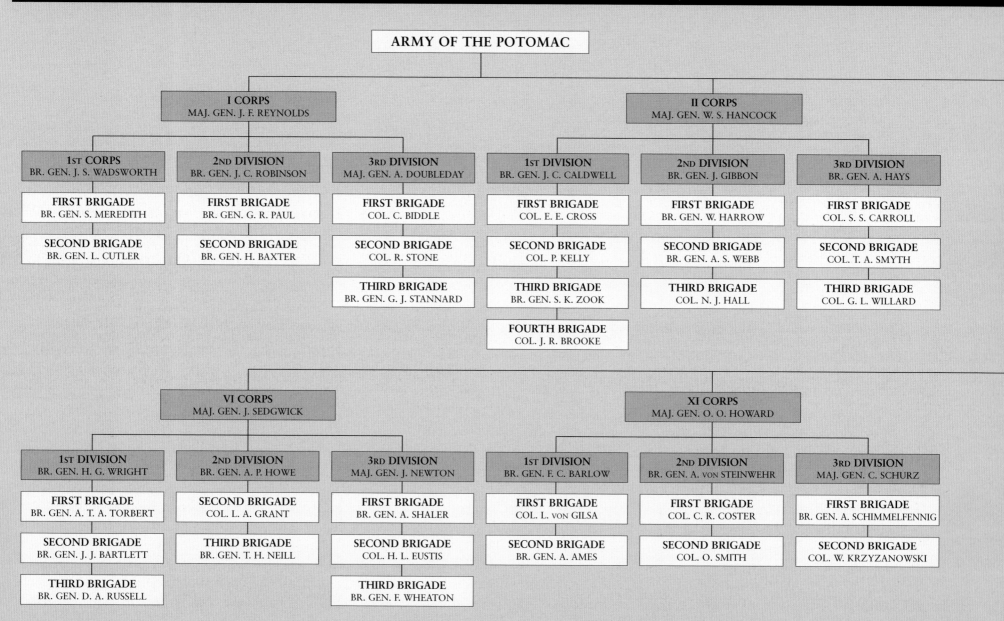

ARMY OF THE POTOMAC

I CORPS
MAJ. GEN. J. F. REYNOLDS

II CORPS
MAJ. GEN. W. S. HANCOCK

1ST CORPS
BR. GEN. J. S. WADSWORTH

2ND DIVISION
BR. GEN. J. C. ROBINSON

3RD DIVISION
MAJ. GEN. A. DOUBLEDAY

1ST DIVISION
BR. GEN. J. C. CALDWELL

2ND DIVISION
BR. GEN. J. GIBBON

3RD DIVISION
BR. GEN. A. HAYS

FIRST BRIGADE
BR. GEN. S. MEREDITH

FIRST BRIGADE
BR. GEN. G. R. PAUL

FIRST BRIGADE
COL. C. BIDDLE

FIRST BRIGADE
COL. E. E. CROSS

FIRST BRIGADE
BR. GEN. W. HARROW

FIRST BRIGADE
COL. S. S. CARROLL

SECOND BRIGADE
BR. GEN. L. CUTLER

SECOND BRIGADE
BR. GEN. H. BAXTER

SECOND BRIGADE
COL. R. STONE

SECOND BRIGADE
COL. P. KELLY

SECOND BRIGADE
BR. GEN. A. S. WEBB

SECOND BRIGADE
COL. T. A. SMYTH

THIRD BRIGADE
BR. GEN. G. J. STANNARD

THIRD BRIGADE
BR. GEN. S. K. ZOOK

THIRD BRIGADE
COL. N. J. HALL

THIRD BRIGADE
COL. G. L. WILLARD

FOURTH BRIGADE
COL. J. R. BROOKE

VI CORPS
MAJ. GEN. J. SEDGWICK

XI CORPS
MAJ. GEN. O. O. HOWARD

1ST DIVISION
BR. GEN. H. G. WRIGHT

2ND DIVISION
BR. GEN. A. P. HOWE

3RD DIVISION
MAJ. GEN. J. NEWTON

1ST DIVISION
BR. GEN. F. C. BARLOW

2ND DIVISION
BR. GEN. A. von STEINWEHR

3RD DIVISION
MAJ. GEN. C. SCHURZ

FIRST BRIGADE
BR. GEN. A. T. A. TORBERT

SECOND BRIGADE
COL. L. A. GRANT

FIRST BRIGADE
BR. GEN. A. SHALER

FIRST BRIGADE
COL. L. von GILSA

FIRST BRIGADE
COL. C. R. COSTER

FIRST BRIGADE
BR. GEN. A. SCHIMMELFENNIG

SECOND BRIGADE
BR. GEN. J. J. BARTLETT

THIRD BRIGADE
BR. GEN. T. H. NEILL

SECOND BRIGADE
COL. H. L. EUSTIS

SECOND BRIGADE
BR. GEN. A. AMES

SECOND BRIGADE
COL. O. SMITH

SECOND BRIGADE
COL. W. KRZYZANOWSKI

THIRD BRIGADE
BR. GEN. D. A. RUSSELL

THIRD BRIGADE
BR. GEN. F. WHEATON

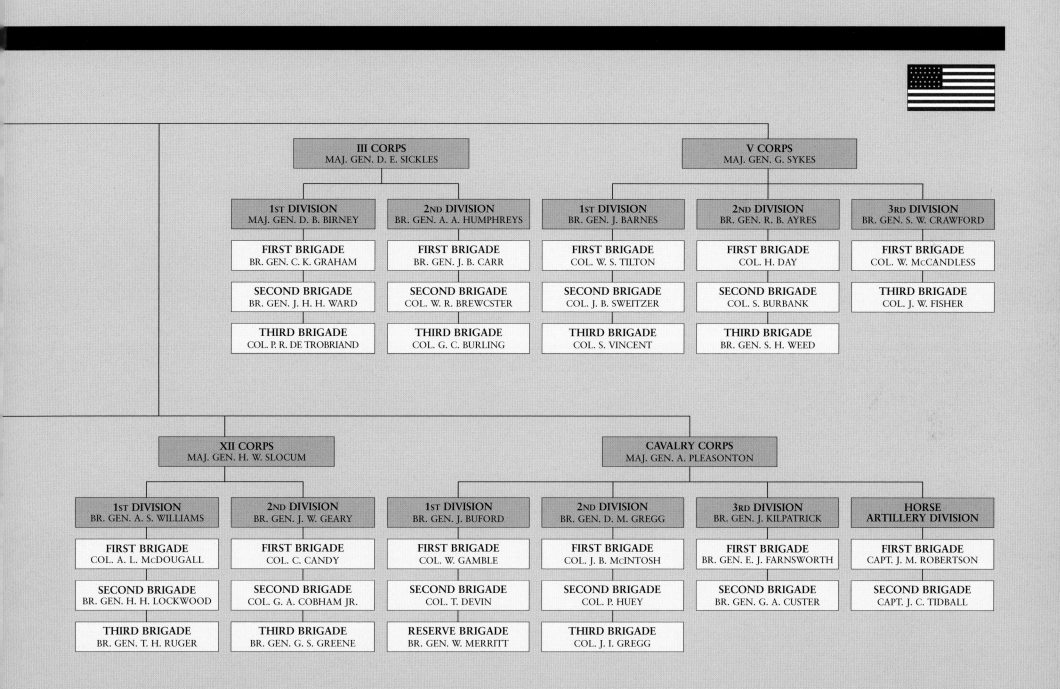

III CORPS
MAJ. GEN. D. E. SICKLES

V CORPS
MAJ. GEN. G. SYKES

III CORPS

1ST DIVISION	2ND DIVISION
MAJ. GEN. D. B. BIRNEY	BR. GEN. A. A. HUMPHREYS

FIRST BRIGADE	FIRST BRIGADE
BR. GEN. C. K. GRAHAM	BR. GEN. J. B. CARR

SECOND BRIGADE	SECOND BRIGADE
BR. GEN. J. H. H. WARD	COL. W. R. BREWCSTER

THIRD BRIGADE	THIRD BRIGADE
COL. P. R. DE TROBRIAND	COL. G. C. BURLING

V CORPS

1ST DIVISION	2ND DIVISION	3RD DIVISION
BR. GEN. J. BARNES	BR. GEN. R. B. AYRES	BR. GEN. S. W. CRAWFORD

FIRST BRIGADE	FIRST BRIGADE	FIRST BRIGADE
COL. W. S. TILTON	COL. H. DAY	COL. W. McCANDLESS

SECOND BRIGADE	SECOND BRIGADE	THIRD BRIGADE
COL. J. B. SWEITZER	COL. S. BURBANK	COL. J. W. FISHER

THIRD BRIGADE	THIRD BRIGADE
COL. S. VINCENT	BR. GEN. S. H. WEED

XII CORPS
MAJ. GEN. H. W. SLOCUM

CAVALRY CORPS
MAJ. GEN. A. PLEASONTON

XII CORPS

1ST DIVISION	2ND DIVISION
BR. GEN. A. S. WILLIAMS	BR. GEN. J. W. GEARY

FIRST BRIGADE	FIRST BRIGADE
COL. A. L. McDOUGALL	COL. C. CANDY

SECOND BRIGADE	SECOND BRIGADE
BR. GEN. H. H. LOCKWOOD	COL. G. A. COBHAM JR.

THIRD BRIGADE	THIRD BRIGADE
BR. GEN. T. H. RUGER	BR. GEN. G. S. GREENE

CAVALRY CORPS

1ST DIVISION	2ND DIVISION	3RD DIVISION	HORSE ARTILLERY DIVISION
BR. GEN. J. BUFORD	BR. GEN. D. M. GREGG	BR. GEN. J. KILPATRICK	

FIRST BRIGADE	FIRST BRIGADE	FIRST BRIGADE	FIRST BRIGADE
COL. W. GAMBLE	COL. J. B. McINTOSH	BR. GEN. E. J. FARNSWORTH	CAPT. J. M. ROBERTSON

SECOND BRIGADE	SECOND BRIGADE	SECOND BRIGADE	SECOND BRIGADE
COL. T. DEVIN	COL. P. HUEY	BR. GEN. G. A. CUSTER	CAPT. J. C. TIDBALL

RESERVE BRIGADE	THIRD BRIGADE
BR. GEN. W. MERRITT	COL. J. I. GREGG

ORDER OF BATTLE: CONFEDERATE STATES ARMY

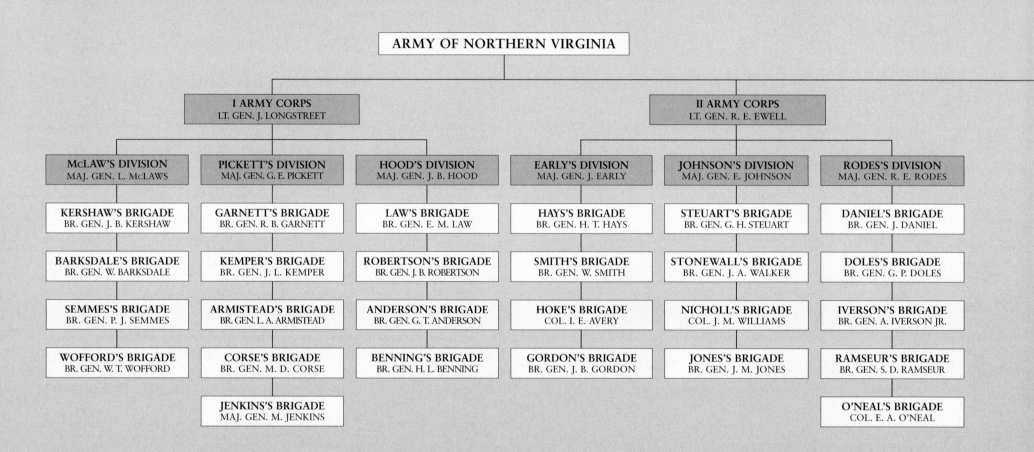

ARMY OF NORTHERN VIRGINIA

I ARMY CORPS
LT. GEN. J. LONGSTREET

II ARMY CORPS
LT. GEN. R. E. EWELL

McLAW'S DIVISION
MAJ. GEN. L. McLAWS

PICKETT'S DIVISION
MAJ. GEN. G. E. PICKETT

HOOD'S DIVISION
MAJ. GEN. J. B. HOOD

EARLY'S DIVISION
MAJ. GEN. J. EARLY

JOHNSON'S DIVISION
MAJ. GEN. E. JOHNSON

RODES'S DIVISION
MAJ. GEN. R. E, RODES

KERSHAW'S BRIGADE
BR. GEN. J. B. KERSHAW

GARNETT'S BRIGADE
BR. GEN. R. B. GARNETT

LAW'S BRIGADE
BR. GEN. E. M. LAW

HAYS'S BRIGADE
BR. GEN. H. T. HAYS

STEUART'S BRIGADE
BR. GEN. G. H. STEUART

DANIEL'S BRIGADE
BR. GEN. J. DANIEL

BARKSDALE'S BRIGADE
BR. GEN. W. BARKSDALE

KEMPER'S BRIGADE
BR. GEN. J. L. KEMPER

ROBERTSON'S BRIGADE
BR. GEN. J. B. ROBERTSON

SMITH'S BRIGADE
BR. GEN. W. SMITH

STONEWALL'S BRIGADE
BR. GEN. J. A. WALKER

DOLES'S BRIGADE
BR. GEN. G. P. DOLES

SEMMES'S BRIGADE
BR. GEN. P. J. SEMMES

ARMISTEAD'S BRIGADE
BR. GEN. L. A. ARMISTEAD

ANDERSON'S BRIGADE
BR. GEN. G. T. ANDERSON

HOKE'S BRIGADE
COL. I. E. AVERY

NICHOLL'S BRIGADE
COL. J. M. WILLIAMS

IVERSON'S BRIGADE
BR. GEN. A. IVERSON JR.

WOFFORD'S BRIGADE
BR. GEN. W. T. WOFFORD

CORSE'S BRIGADE
BR. GEN. M. D. CORSE

BENNING'S BRIGADE
BR. GEN. H. L. BENNING

GORDON'S BRIGADE
BR. GEN. J. B. GORDON

JONES'S BRIGADE
BR. GEN. J. M. JONES

RAMSEUR'S BRIGADE
BR. GEN. S. D. RAMSEUR

JENKINS'S BRIGADE
MAJ. GEN. M. JENKINS

O'NEAL'S BRIGADE
COL. E. A. O'NEAL

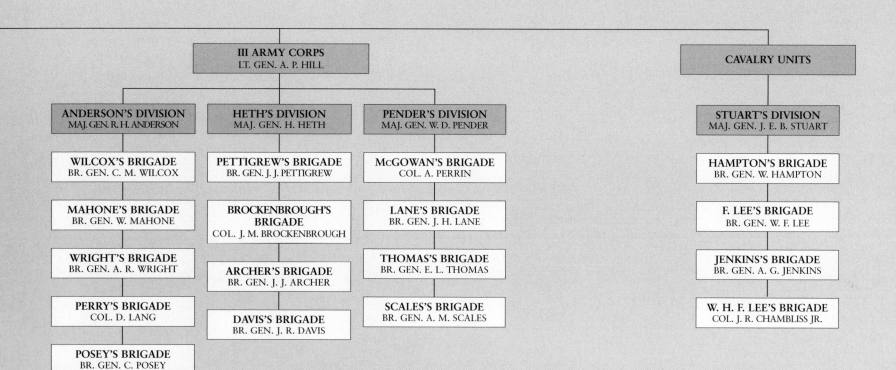

III ARMY CORPS
LT. GEN. A. P. HILL

CAVALRY UNITS

ANDERSON'S DIVISION
MAJ. GEN. R. H. ANDERSON

HETH'S DIVISION
MAJ. GEN. H. HETH

PENDER'S DIVISION
MAJ. GEN. W. D. PENDER

STUART'S DIVISION
MAJ. GEN. J. E. B. STUART

WILCOX'S BRIGADE
BR. GEN. C. M. WILCOX

PETTIGREW'S BRIGADE
BR. GEN. J. J. PETTIGREW

McGOWAN'S BRIGADE
COL. A. PERRIN

HAMPTON'S BRIGADE
BR. GEN. W. HAMPTON

MAHONE'S BRIGADE
BR. GEN. W. MAHONE

BROCKENBROUGH'S BRIGADE
COL. J. M. BROCKENBROUGH

LANE'S BRIGADE
BR. GEN. J. H. LANE

F. LEE'S BRIGADE
BR. GEN. W. F. LEE

WRIGHT'S BRIGADE
BR. GEN. A. R. WRIGHT

ARCHER'S BRIGADE
BR. GEN. J. J. ARCHER

THOMAS'S BRIGADE
BR. GEN. E. L. THOMAS

JENKINS'S BRIGADE
BR. GEN. A. G. JENKINS

PERRY'S BRIGADE
COL. D. LANG

DAVIS'S BRIGADE
BR. GEN. J. R. DAVIS

SCALES'S BRIGADE
BR. GEN. A. M. SCALES

W. H. F. LEE'S BRIGADE
COL. J. R. CHAMBLISS JR.

POSEY'S BRIGADE
BR. GEN. C. POSEY

BIBLIOGRAPHY

Clark, Champ. *Gettysburg: The Confederate High Tide*. Alexandria, VA: Time-Life Books, 1985.

Commager, Henry Steele, ed. *The Blue and the Gray: The Story of the Civil War as Told by Participants*. New York: Mentor, 1973 (paperback).

Dougherty, Kevin. *Great Commanders Head-to-Head: The Battles of the Civil War*. San Diego, CA: Thunder Bay Press, 2009.

Foote, Shelby. *The Civil War: A Narrative*. Vol. 2, *Fredericksburg to Meridian*. New York: Random House, 1986.

Frassanito, William A. *Gettysburg: A Journey in Time*. New York: Scribner's, 1975.

Freeman, Douglas S. *Lee's Lieutenants: A Study in Command*. 3 vols. New York: Charles Scribner's Sons, 1942–1944.

Freeman, Douglas S. *R. E. Lee: A Biography*. 4 vols. New York: Charles Scribner's Sons, 1934.

Longstreet, James. *From Manassas to Appomattox*. Secaucus, NJ: Blue and Grey Press, 1984.

Sears, Stephen. *Gettysburg*. New York: Houghton Mifflin Co, 2003.

Shaara, Michael. *Killer Angels*. New York: Ballantine Books, 1975.

Tucker, Glenn. *High Tide at Gettysburg*. New York: Smithmark, 1994.

Warner, Ezra. *Generals in Blue*. Baton Rouge, LA: Louisiana State University Press, 1964.

Warner, Ezra. *Generals in Gray*. Baton Rouge, LA: Louisiana State University Press, 1959.

Picture Credits

INDEX

Page numbers in *italics* refer to illustrations and maps.

THE GETTYSBURG ADDRESS

DELIVERED BY ABRAHAM LINCOLN NOV. 19 1863

AT THE DEDICATION SERVICES ON THE BATTLE FIELD

Fourscore and seven years ago our fathers brought forth on this continent a new nation, conceived in liberty, and dedicated to the proposition that all men are created equal. ★ ★ ★ Now we are engaged in a great civil war, testing whether that nation, or any nation so conceived and so dedicated, can long endure. ★ ★ We are met on a great battle-field of that war. ★ We